Makers
of the
Modern
World

Nikola Pašić and Ante Trumbić
The Kingdom of Serbs, Croats and Slovenes
Dejan Djokić

HH
HAUS HISTORIES

First published in Great Britain in 2010 by
Haus Publishing Ltd
70 Cadogan Place
London SW1X 9AH
www.hauspublishing.com

Copyright © Dejan Djokić, 2010

The moral right of the author has been asserted

A CIP catalogue record for this book
is available from the British Library

ISBN 978-1-905791-78-1

Series design by Susan Buchanan
Typeset in Sabon by MacGuru Ltd
Printed in Dubai by Oriental Press
Map by Martin Lubikowski, ML Design, London

To the memory of Vane Ivanović and Desimir Tošić,
and to Stevan K Pavlowitch

Contents

Note on Spelling and Pronunciation

All former-Yugoslav personal and place names are spelled in their original form, unless there exist commonly accepted anglicised spellings and except in direct citations where other authors use different spellings. Therefore, it is Belgrade, not Beograd, but Niš, not Nish. The following exceptions have been made:

a) I have generally used Fiume, rather than the modern (Croatian) spelling Rijeka, since the Italian name of the Adriatic port was commonly used at the time of the Paris Peace Conference. I provide both Serbo-Croat/Slovene and 'foreign' place names wherever appropriate.
b) I have anglicised only the names of Yugoslav monarchs, so it is King *Nicholas* of Montenegro, but *Nikola* Pašić.

The following is a brief guide to pronunciation in the language formerly known as Serbo-Croat and in Slovene:

c – 'ts' as in nets
č – 'ch' as in charming
ć – softer than č, close to 'tu' as in tuna

dj (also spelled as đ) – 'j' as in juice

dž – harder than 'dj', 'j' as in jogging

j – 'y' as in Yugoslavia

lj – no corresponding English sound, but remotely similar to 'lu' as in solution

nj – similar to 'n' as in new

r – pronounced similarly to the Scottish rolling 'r'

š – 'sh' as in shy

ž – 'su' as in pleasure

Preface and Acknowledgements

This book tells the complex, but fascinating, story of the Yugoslav delegation at the Paris Peace Conference of 1919–20. It centres on the difficult relationship between the delegation's two leading figures – Nikola Pašić and Ante Trumbić – and the main challenge they and their country faced in Paris: securing the recognition of the Kingdom of Serbs, Croats and Slovenes by the Allies within internationally-recognised borders. The story of Pašić, Trumbić and the Serb-Croat-Slovene delegation at the Peace Conference is placed in a wider historical framework. It is hoped, therefore, that the book will be of use to readers interested in the origins and making of Yugoslavia as well as those with an interest in modern Balkan history.

Part I of the book deals with Yugoslav history prior to the fateful events of 1919–20. The reader is introduced to the South Slav lands and peoples, in particular Serbia and the Serbs and Croatia and the Croats, while the origins of the Yugoslav idea, which emerged in the 19th century, are traced simultaneously. The lives and careers of the two main protagonists, Pašić and Trumbić, up to 1919 are also described in this part of the book.

In Part II the reader is first introduced to the delegation of the Kingdom of Serbs, Croats and Slovenes at the Peace Conference: its key personnel, its structure, its main aims and the most serious obstacles it faced. The story then moves on to the first six months of the Conference, which proved to be most important and eventful, not just from the Yugoslav point of view. Between the opening session of the Conference on 18 January 1919 and the signing of the Peace Treaty with Germany at Versailles on 28 June, the Yugoslavs managed to achieve international recognition of their country, but not to agree on borders with most of their neighbours, notably Italy. The Adriatic question – undoubtedly the most serious problem the delegation had to deal with – is treated in a separate chapter, as is the question of war crimes and war guilt.

Once the German Treaty had been signed, the remaining issues were regarded by the leaders of Britain, France and the US as relatively minor. However, for the Yugoslavs the struggle to reach border settlements with most of their neighbours continued. The remainder of this part explains how events unfolded during the rest of the Conference and to what extent the Yugoslavs' main goals were achieved. In addition to external pressures, divisions within the delegation, especially differences between Pašić and Trumbić, are explored, as are differences between the delegation and the government in Belgrade and the Allies in Paris.

The final section of the book, Part III, deals with the legacy of the Paris Peace Conference in inter-war Yugoslavia and explains how the political careers of Pašić and Trumbić developed after they returned from Paris. This part also reflects on the achievements and failures of Yugoslavia, ninety years after it made its international debut in Paris and nearly twenty years after its violent break-up.

ooooo

I am grateful to my commissioning editor Jaqueline Mitchell, to Barbara Schwepcke, my publisher, and to Professor Alan Sharp, the series editor, for the faith they showed in me and for their support and patience while I was working on this manuscript. This book stands on the foundations provided by two doyens of Yugoslav history: the late Professor Ivo J Lederer and Professor Andrej Mitrović, who wrote the pioneering histories of Yugoslavia's participation at the Paris Peace Conference (see Further Reading for bibliographical details). The present work is different in aim and scope, but will be, I hope, read alongside these two classics, as well as being more accessible to a general, non-academic audience.

Preliminary research for this book was carried out while I was on study leave funded by the Arts and Humanities Research Council – the AHRC grant is hereby gratefully acknowledged. I should like to thank the staff at the British Library, London, where most of the research and writing was done, and my colleagues in the Department of History at Goldsmiths College, University of London, for their support and understanding of my research commitments. I have learnt much about early 20th-century Serbia and Yugoslavia from discussions with Professor Mitrović and with Professor Ljubinka Trgovčević – his wife and an expert on the subject in her own right. When in Belgrade, I have especially benefited from conversations with Dr Aleksa Djilas, whose erudition is matched only by his and his wife Olgica's hospitality. Dr Predrag Marković of the Institute for Contemporary History in Belgrade has helped me shape some arguments in the book with his characteristically intelligent comments and suggestions. Last, but not least, I am grateful to the Popović-Gojković family for providing me with a home in London in more than one way.

My whole career as an academic historian, and thus this book, too, may not have been possible without the support and inspiration of three Yugoslav friends, two of whom are sadly no longer alive: Ivan Stevan (Vane) Ivanović (1913–99), Desimir Tošić (1920–2008), and Stevan K Pavlowitch. One was in Paris as a small boy during the Peace Conference, close relatives of two of them were direct participants, while the lives of all three were shaped by the events of 1919–20.

Vane Ivanović was one of the first and the last true Yugoslavs, an Anglophile philanthropist born into a Croat-Serb family whose members helped found the Kingdom of Serbs, Croats and Slovenes. His father and uncle were prominent pro-Yugoslav politicians in the late Habsburg Monarchy; Božo Banac, a maritime expert in the Yugoslav delegation at the Peace Conference, would become his stepfather. The six-year-old Vane was in Paris at the time of the Conference. His father did not participate in the work of the Yugoslav delegation, but had moved temporarily to the French capital to impress his beautiful young wife and to buy a car. He bought a Winton Six, but the marriage did not last.

Desimir Tošić was born when the Paris Conference was in its second year, the Italo-Yugoslav dispute over the eastern Adriatic still unresolved, and the Hungarian and Ottoman Turkish Treaties yet to be signed. A child of the inter-war period, imprisoned by the Nazis during the Second World War, and a political émigré in Paris and London during the Cold War, he was a prominent advocate of democracy and a critic of nationalism during the Yugoslav War of the 1990s, which undid much of what had been achieved in Paris. Tošić, who had always declared himself a Serb, but who had lamented Yugoslavia, had spent most of his life writing about the country, especially the Serb-Croat 'question' of the inter-war period, which began to emerge at the time of the Conference.

Last, but not least, Professor Stevan K Pavlowitch, a British-based Francophile academic born in the Kingdom of Yugoslavia, has taught me more than anyone else about Yugoslavia and about being a critical historian (but should not be held accountable for my shortcomings as a scholar). His grandfather, and namesake, was at the Paris Peace Conference as Trumbić's secretary; there with him were his wife and three children – Professor Pavlowitch's father, uncle and aunt. Stevan K Pavlowitch (the historian) kindly lent me the diary of Stevan K Pavlowitch (the diplomat) and shared with me everything he remembers of his grandfather's recollections of Paris. On one occasion, he even telephoned his uncle, born in Paris during the First World War and now living in Belgrade,* to check some facts. Professor Pavlowitch also read the final manuscript, offered characteristically insightful comments and improved the language and style. Needless to say, I bear the sole responsibility for any remaining errors.

The book is dedicated to these three unconventional Yugoslavs, whose visions of Yugoslavia would have probably met with approval by Trumbić (at least the Trumbić of 1919–20), though possibly not by Pašić.

Dejan Djokić
London, 28 August 2009

---

* Sadly, Dobroslav St. Pavlović died just days after this book was completed, aged 92.

Prelude

Paris, 10 January 1919. Celebrations of the first peacetime New Year in four years over, the city is preparing to host a major international congress that will formally end 'the war to end all wars'. Foreign dignitaries – presidents, monarchs, prime ministers and diplomats – begin to arrive in the French capital, among them those from a new country with a long, but somewhat familiar name: the Kingdom of Serbs, Croats and Slovenes – a state created the previous month by the unification of the kingdoms of Serbia and Montenegro and the formerly Habsburg South Slav provinces, including Bosnia-Herzegovina, Croatia and 'Slovenia'; a state still to be granted external recognition and yet to secure its international borders.[1]

At 10.00 a.m., Nikola Pašić, wartime Prime Minister of Serbia, and Ante Trumbić, a Dalmatian Croat who championed the Yugoslav cause in the West during the war, meet in the Hotel Campbell, Avenue de Friedland. Pašić had checked in at the hotel several days previously, having been appointed head of the Serb-Croat-Slovene delegation for the forthcoming Peace Conference. Trumbić, already in Paris, had been recently appointed Foreign Minister in the young state's provisional government, but remained in the French capital to start preparations for the Peace Conference. He was appointed number two in the delegation.

The two men represent the aims and hopes of the newly-born Yugoslavia (as the country was often referred to even before its name was officially changed to the Kingdom of Yugoslavia in 1929), but also of its constituent parts. Pašić is an embodiment of pre-Yugoslav Serbia, Trumbić a symbol of pre-Yugoslav Croatia. The two men bring together the different historical and cultural traditions of the lands and the peoples they represent. They symbolise nationalist aspirations of the past, present and future: Serb, Croat *and* Yugoslav. Bringing these different visions and hopes together under a common umbrella in early December 1918 was a major achievement. Keeping them united and moulding them into a coherent identity was an even greater challenge. Were the Yugoslav founders and peacemakers – the *Yugomakers* – up to the task?

Also present at what is the first session of the Yugoslav peace delegation are Milenko Vesnić, Belgrade's minister to Paris, General Petar Pešić, head of the military section of the delegation, and two former Habsburg Yugoslav politicians, Otokar Ribarž (sometimes spelled Rybář) and Ante Tresić-Pavičić. Minutes are taken by Ninko Perić.[2] Vesnić and Perić are members of Pašić's People's Radical Party. The Radicals and General Pešić are all Serbs, Trumbić and Tresić-Pavičić are Croats, while Ribarž is a Slovene.

What Pašić has to say does not sound too promising. He informs the delegates that Stéphen Pichon, the French Foreign Minister, had told him the previous day it was unlikely that the Yugoslavs would be allowed to send more than three delegates to sessions of the Conference. Pašić had demanded that they should be allowed to have five, and certainly no less than four, delegates. Similarly, General Pešić's news does not bode well. He reports his conversation with a senior officer close to Marshal Ferdinand Foch, the wartime commander of the Allied armies, who thought the Yugoslavs' demands in the north-east Adriatic were unlikely to be met, since Italy would not agree to the old Austrian-Italian border. Trumbić, who as a Dalmatian is intimately concerned with the outcome of a settlement with Italy, is particularly worried. He suggests that urgent action is needed, and that leading experts in the field of finance and commercial shipping from all parts of the new country, not just Serbia, should be summoned immediately and included in the work of the delegation.

Over the next few days matters take a turn for the worse from the Yugoslav point of view. The Big Four – Britain, France, Italy and the United States of America – propose that Belgrade be allocated only two seats at the Conference meetings. More significantly, due to Italy's opposition, the Conference does not recognise the Kingdom of Serbs, Croats and Slovenes. The delegation would be allowed to take part, but as the delegation of the Kingdom of Serbia, while there would also be one seat reserved for the Kingdom of Montenegro. This means not only that the proclamation of the Kingdom of Serbs, Croats and Slovenes in Belgrade on 1 December 1918 is not recognised by the Yugoslavs' main allies, but that even the unification of Serbia and Montenegro of late November, opposed by the exiled Montenegrin King Nicholas and his supporters, has effectively been rejected by the Powers.

The Allies' decisions pose several serious problems for the Yugoslavs. They expose the new country's precarious international predicament and bring to the surface internal divisions, mostly, though not exclusively, between Pašić and the

Serb members and Trumbić and the Croat members. The divisions in Paris in many ways reflect the lines of political conflict that begin to appear back home and will go on to destabilise inter-war Yugoslavia.

The question of how many delegates should represent Yugoslavia went beyond the issue of Serbia's pride: as a victorious power that suffered extremely heavy losses in the war, the Serb-Croat-Slovene Kingdom should be entitled at least the same number of seats as a country such as Brazil (three) – so the Yugoslavs thought. (In the event, the Allies agreed to confer three seats on Belgium and 'Serbia', in recognition of their contribution to the war effort, while Montenegro's chair would remain empty through the Conference.) That way each one of the three constituent groups making up the Yugoslav nation could be represented at the Conference.

In other words, the Yugoslavs had hoped that in addition to Pašić (a Serb) and Trumbić (a Croat), a Slovene representative would be able to attend. Sending only Pašić and Trumbić to the Conference sessions would risk disappointing the Slovenes, already feeling insecure due to the Italian threat in the north-east Adriatic. Moreover, a Slovene delegate could act as a buffer between Pašić and Trumbić, whose mutual antagonism was obvious. The two men were brought together by the same ideal: the unification and international recognition of Yugoslavia. Yet, their differences, going back to the war years, could not be disguised, and often threatened to undermine the work of the delegation.

The Yugoslav delegation debates for two days how to word a reply to the Allied decisions. Trumbić thinks they should insist on the immediate recognition of the Kingdom of Serbs, Croats and Slovenes and also on the delegation being granted three seats. Pašić agrees, but believes these to be two separate issues that should be dealt with accordingly. It seems as if Pašić and the Serbs are not too upset by the failure of the Powers to grant an immediate recognition of the Serbo-Croat-Slovene state. General Pešić's objection to Trumbić's referring to 'former Serbia' in his draft reply – 'as if Serbia does not exist anymore … Austria-Hungary may be former, but Serbia is not'[3] – gives a clue to the thinking of the Serb delegates.

Pašić and the Serb members of the delegation are loyal to the Yugoslav state and certainly recognise that the Serb-Croat-Slovene Kingdom is a reality, but in their view, so is Serbia. In Serbia Pašić sees not just the South Slavs' liberator and unifier, but also the core of the new state. The creation of Yugoslavia need not mean the end of Serbia's existence; rather, it could represent the culmination of a century-long struggle for the liberation and unification of Serbs – and eventually Croats and Slovenes. Trumbić, on the other hand, views Yugoslavia as a new country, a successor state to Austria-Hungary as well as to Serbia. Ironically, while Pašić was in favour of political centralism at home, he preferred the 'three-part' name for the country – Kingdom of Serbs, Croats and Slovenes – with 'Serbs' mentioned first. Trumbić, in favour of a decentralised government, believed that the country should be called simply 'Yugoslavia'.

The first few meetings of the delegation reveal the major challenges the Yugoslavs would face in Paris, namely the uncertainty over the extent of the Powers' support and the tensions between Pašić and Trumbić. The latter in many ways reflects the uneasy relationship between Serbia, a victorious ally, and the formerly Habsburg – and thus enemy – lands that joined together to form a single political entity for the first time in history. The antagonism between Pašić and Trumbić stemmed above all from their personal and political differences. That the two men happened also to be a leading Serb and a leading Croat politician was unfortunate. For the initial political conflict, both at home and among the members of the delegation, would gradually transform into a Serb-Croat rivalry. This conflict dominated inter-war Yugoslavia, even though it represented but one dimension of the country's political contest.[4]

Nikola Pašić

I

The Lives and the Lands

1

Who were the Yugoslavs?

The Yugoslav delegation in Paris sought to achieve more than just the recognition of Yugoslavia's borders. It also hoped to secure international backing for the national self-determination of the South Slavs and official recognition of the Serb-Croat-Slovene Kingdom. The main ideological 'justification' for the creation of Yugoslavia was that Serbs, Croats and Slovenes were three branches of one ethnic nation which had been divided by foreign imperial powers for centuries. As a leading member of the delegation told his Paris audience in March 1919: 'The Serbs, Croats and Slovenes are descendants of the Slav tribes who came down from the Carpathian regions during the early centuries of our era and were all of them completely akin to one another [...] the Jugoslav nation has hammered out for itself an invincible national soul. Oft-repeated persecutions decimated its upper classes, its nobles, men of letters, priests, burgesses; to massacres were added all possible methods of denationalisation, and the peasantry, the last bulwark of the nation, was reduced to a state of veritable political slavery. And yet this proud race, deprived of its leaders and of every external means of intellectual development, found within itself, in spite of all repressive measures, not only the means of subsistence, but also of progress. Jealously and successfully, it preserved intact and pure its language and national conscience, its ethnic unity which nothing could shake, – not the Great Schism between Rome and Constantinople, not the gulf which elsewhere separates the followers of Christianity from the True Believers of the Prophet. Islam was adopted by a million Jugoslavs who nevertheless remained true to the language and national conscience of their ancestors. Everywhere else in Europe the dividing line between the Greek and Roman Churches corresponds to an ethnic line of demarcation. In the Jugoslav territory, which it cuts in half, it has not injured the national unity even in the slightest degree.'[1]

How much 'truth' was there in this official interpretation of the Yugoslav history?

Understanding Yugoslavia

It is not easy to understand Yugoslavia, the former land of the South Slavs. There are today seven officially acknowledged South Slavonic nations: Bosniaks (or Bosnian Muslims), Bulgarians, Croats, Macedonians, Montenegrins, Slovenians and Serbs. However, some would argue that there are only four, five or six South Slav nations. Many Serbs (and Montenegrins) believe that Montenegrins are Serbs, while some Croats and some Serbs claim that Bosniaks are not a separate nation, but really are Serbs and/or Croats who converted to Islam during the long period of Ottoman rule in the Balkans (between the mid-14th and the early 20th centuries). To many Bulgarians, Macedonians are but a branch of their nation. There are also declared 'Yugoslavs', though there are not many of them left today, who would argue that they form a separate nation and/or that Serbs, Croats, Bosniaks and Montenegrins are ethnically the same.

What is indisputable is that all those nations listed above – with the notable exception of Bulgarians – lived in Yugoslavia, a country which existed between late 1918 and late 1991/early 1992. Between 1918 and 1941, Yugoslavia was formally a nation-state of the 'three-named' (triune) Yugoslav nation, divided into three 'tribes': Serbs, Croats and Slovenes. Indeed, the original name for the country between 1918 and 1929 was the Kingdom of Serbs, Croats and Slovenes. In 1929, King Alexander renamed the country 'Yugoslavia' in order to symbolise his integralist Yugoslav project. Between 1941 and 1945, the country was occupied and partitioned by the Axis powers. However, there was a Yugoslav king (Alexander's young son Peter II) and a government-in-exile, while in the country itself two resistance movements (some would say one) fought for the restoration of a Yugoslavia. At the end of the Second World War a communist-dominated government led by Marshal Josip Broz Tito restored the state and transformed it into a socialist federation.

The three inter-war 'tribes' were then upgraded to 'nations'. In addition to Serbs, Croats and Slovenes, Macedonians and Montenegrins were also recognised as separate nations; in the inter-war period Montenegrins were regarded and many regarded themselves as Serbs, while Macedonians were 'southern Serbs' although most of them did not feel Serbian. Nominally, each nation was given a republic within Yugoslavia. The Yugoslav federation was initially made up of five nations and six republics. Bosnia-Herzegovina was the sixth republic – alongside Slovenia, Croatia, Serbia, Montenegro and Macedonia – but Bosnian Muslims were not recognised by that republic's constitution as a separate nation until 1968 (and as late as 1974 at the federal level).

The South Slavs speak closely-related languages; but again, there is no agreement on how many languages they actually speak, nor what these languages should be called. In inter-war Yugoslavia there was one official language: Serbo-Croat-Slovene. After the Second World War, Slovenes spoke Slovene, and Macedonians Macedonian, a language 'created' in 1946 from a dialect deemed least close to Bulgarian and Serbian. The population of the four central republics spoke Serbo-Croat, which most Croats simply called Croatian and most Serbs and Montenegrins Serbian. Bosnians, especially Muslims, usually called it Serbo-Croat. In areas where significant non-Yugoslav minorities lived, their languages were also in official use: Italian in Istria and Dalmatia, Hungarian in Vojvodina, and Albanian in Kosovo and Macedonia. Around 500,000 ethnic Germans, who lived mostly in Vojvodina, were expelled at the end of the Second World War. (Vojvodina and Kosovo were two autonomous provinces within the Republic of Serbia. Kosovo and Metohija was initially an autonomous 'region' – lower in the hierarchy than a 'province'.)

With the dissolution of Yugoslavia, the Serbo-Croat language disintegrated as well, so there are now three, possibly four, successor languages: Bosnian, Croatian and Serbian, and latterly Montenegrin. Most linguists, however, agree that this is still the same language. To make things even more complex, different dialects spoken across the linguistic territory of Serbo-Croat do not correspond with ethnic boundaries. Croatian and Slovenian in particular contain numerous, relatively distinct dialects. Slovenians and Macedonians speak languages clearly distinguishable from former Serbo-Croat, but some Bulgarians – and possibly some

Macedonians – believe that Macedonian is but a dialect of Bulgarian. Anyway, it is hard to draw a clear linguistic line in a largely coherent South Slavonic territory that stretches from the Slovenian Alps to the Bulgarian Black Sea, with languages and dialects merging into each other. The makers of Yugoslavia in Paris were aware of this, and they used the 'linguistic argument' to support their claims. Although he demanded (or perhaps because he demanded) parts of Bulgarian territory for Yugoslavia, and although he believed the Bulgarians bore collective guilt for the war, Nikola Pašić, leader of the Yugoslav delegation at the Paris Peace Conference, declared during the Conference that he hoped Bulgaria would eventually join the South Slav union.[2]

Historical legacy

Such a complex picture emerged out of the historical legacy of the region. South Slavs, together with East Slavs (Russians, Ukrainians, Belorusians, Ruthenians) and West Slavs (Poles, Czechs, Slovaks, Lusatian Serbs) belong to a large Slavonic family. They migrated into the Balkans in the 6th and 7th centuries from areas that today form parts of Poland, Germany and Ukraine. Among numerous small tribes two stood out, even though they were not always distinguished by contemporary non-Slav observers: Serbs and Croats. Croats settled in western parts of the Balkan peninsula, more or less in today's Croatia and Bosnia; Serbs to the east of them, roughly in present-day Herzegovina, south-west Serbia and Montenegro. Bulgarians were originally an Asiatic tribe that settled to the east of the Serbs and merged with local Slavonic tribes, becoming completely slavonicised but retaining the original name. A similar mixing of Slavs and non-Slavs may have occurred with the Serbs and Croats prior to their settlement in the Balkans, but in any case, by the time they settled in south-east Europe, they had been long slavonicised. The Slav settlers mixed with Illyrians, Vlachs and other indigenous Balkan populations and with other migrants, who included Celts and Romans.

The South Slavs converted to Christianity by the 9th century. A special alphabet, loosely based on the Greek, was invented by two priests from Salonica, Cyril and Methodius – which their pupils further developed into Cyrillic – and was used to translate the Bible into Slavonic. Because of their geographic position, Bulgarians and Serbs came under the influence of Constantinople, while Croats were closer to Rome. After the 'Great Schism' of 1054, Serbs and Bulgarians became Orthodox while Croats belonged to the Roman Catholic Church, although the fault line was not as fixed then as it appears now. For example, the first Serbian kings sought recognition from both Constantinople and Rome, while Croats sometimes used Cyrillic (as well as a related Glagolitic alphabet), traditionally associated with Orthodox Slavs such as Bulgarians, Russians and Serbs.

During the Middle Ages the South Slavs founded several independent kingdoms and empires: Bulgaria, Croatia, Rascia (present-day south-western Serbia), Zeta (in present-day Montenegro), and Bosnia. Rascia and Zeta formed the basis of a united Serbian kingdom that grew into a powerful regional empire in the 14th century. The Crown of Croatia merged with the Crown of Hungary in the early 12th century, which meant in reality the beginning of centuries of subjugation to Hungarian and, from the 16th century, Austrian rule. After initially being part of a large Slav entity in the early Middle Ages, Slovenes came under Austrian control, while the territory of the present-day Macedonian republic was part of the Byzantine, Bulgarian, and Serbian Empires throughout the Middle Ages. Habsburg and Ottoman conquests meant that by the mid-15th century most South Slavs were under foreign rule. The exceptions were the city-state of Dubrovnik (Ragusa) and tiny Montenegro (in the territory of Zeta), ruled by native Prince-Bishops.

The Orthodox Slavs also established their own churches during the Middle Ages. The Serbian Orthodox Church was founded in the early 13th century as an autocephalous archbishopric. It became a Patriarchate a century and a half later, and survived the disappearance of the Serbian state, despite being abolished twice, and restored once, by the Ottomans. The founders of a united Serbian state at the end of the 12th century, and of the Serbian church, both came from the Nemanjić dynasty, which ruled Serbia for nearly two centuries. The relationship between State and Church was stronger in the eastern parts of the former Roman Empire than in its western parts, but in the case of Serbia it was particularly strong due to the Nemanjić connection.

The rise of the Serbian Empire coincided with the decline of the Byzantine and Bulgarian Empires, but was halted by the emergence of the Ottoman Turks. Emperor Stefan Dušan's premature death in 1355 led to domestic problems. His young son Stefan Uroš V was not strong enough to keep the different factions together, and the state was internally divided when the Ottomans arrived. They defeated Serbian and Serbian-led armies at several key battles, but the defeat at Kosovo on 28 June 1389, St Vitus' Day, would prove fateful because of the legend which developed in its aftermath. It was on 28 June 1914 that Archduke Franz Ferdinand was assassinated in Sarajevo by Gavrilo Princip, a member of the Young Bosnia nationalist organisation, and it was on 28 June 1919 that the Treaty of Versailles was signed – two events which marked the beginning and the end of the First World War, respectively.

The powerful, if short-lived, medieval empire, the establishment of the independent church, the Holy Nemanjić dynasty (most of its rulers were canonised by the Serbian Church) and the Battle of Kosovo would provide the foundation of Serbian medieval mythology which survived through oral poetry and Church sermons until the 19th century and the birth of nationalism. Gavrilo Princip, Franz Ferdinand's young assassin born in Bosnia of Serb parents, knew all about the historical significance of 28 June. Nikola Pašić was another ardent student of his nation's history. The choice of date for Franz Ferdinand's visit to Bosnia-Herzegovina, which then had a majority of Serbs in its population, was not exactly tactful.

Between the 15th and 18th centuries, parts of Croatia also came under Ottoman Turkish rule. The Croats' collective memories of the independent medieval kingdom survived too, but the end of independence was not as traumatic as in the Serbian case. This was partly because the conquerors – the Hungarians in the 12th century and Austrians in the 16th – were culturally similar to, and shared the religion of, those they conquered. The Ottoman Turks were not only Muslim, they were an Asiatic people whose culture and traditions differed significantly from the nascent Serbian Byzantine-Slav civilisation. Moreover, formally at least, the Croat Crown united with the Hungarian realm, and Croat 'statehood' nominally survived in various legal documents and in the institutions of *sabor* (Diet) and *ban* (governor), even though the Croat nobility, like the Serbian one, mostly perished or lost its Slav identity. Both Serbs and Croats – in common with other neighbouring peoples, such as Hungarians – believed they defended Christian Europe from Islam (the so-called *antemurale Christianitatis* myth).

Bosnia, situated between medieval Croatia and Serbia, briefly grew into a powerful regional kingdom in the 14th century – taking advantage of Serbia's decline – but it too was soon conquered by the Ottomans, as was Herzegovina. It was the only former South Slav state where large-scale conversions to Islam took place. There is no agreement among scholars on why this was so, but it is safe to argue that it had something to do with the lack of a strong national church such as that which existed in Serbia. Unlike Croatia, Bosnia was not an undisputed Roman Catholic territory either. There was a local Bosnian church, which may have been influenced by Bogomilism (a dualist heresy which originated in 10th-century Bulgaria), and certainly was more tolerant of its existence. Conversions offered many advantages, were not always forced, and took place gradually.

The existence of significant numbers of Balkan Muslims is one of two main legacies of imperial rule in the region. The other is large-scale migrations. The 'Great Migration' of 1690 saw tens of thousands of Serbs, led by Patriarch Arsenije Čarnojević, settle in present-day Bosnia, Croatia and northern Serbia. The significance of this, and other similar migrations, is twofold: firstly, many Serbs left their medieval homelands, including present-day Kosovo, creating space for largely Muslim Albanians. Albanians had lived in medieval Serbia, but it is likely their numbers in the region grew following the Serb migrations; some Orthodox Albanians left together with Serbs, gradually becoming serbianised, while some Muslim and Orthodox Serbs who stayed behind became albanianised in due course. Secondly, as a result of the migrations, a large number of Serbs now lived alongside Croats and Bosnians.

The creation of Yugoslavia in 1918 and its emergence onto the international stage in Paris in 1919–20 may therefore be seen as part of the region's imperial legacy (the legacy which has been partly reversed during the Yugoslav wars of the 1940s and the 1990s). The interpretation of pre-1918 history by the founders of Yugoslavia was undoubtedly ideological and intended to serve the new nation's political goals in Paris in 1919. However, it was by no means without foundation.

2
Pašić's Serbia

The beginning of modern Serbian nationalism may be conveniently traced to around 1804, the year peasants of the Belgrade *paşalik* (province) revolted against local Ottoman rule.[1] The revolt started as a social rebellion, but it eventually turned into a struggle for national liberation. Within a few years the Serb insurgents, led by Karadjordje (Black George) Petrović, were in control of what is today central Serbia, including Belgrade. During the First Serbian Uprising (1804–13) a nascent Serbian state was established, with a government and an assembly. The Serbs looked to Russia for military aid, but following the 1812 Treaty of Bucharest, which ended the Russo-Ottoman War, the rebellion was crushed by the Ottomans and Karadjordje forced to flee to Austria.

The Second Serbian Uprising (1815–30) was led by Miloš Obrenović, who had Karadjordje executed as a proof of his alleged loyalty to the Sultan, and who managed to gain autonomy for Serbia by relying more on diplomacy than warfare. He reigned like an Ottoman pasha, but also instituted social changes that marked a break with the Ottoman era (even if that break was not as radical and clear as is often assumed): the Belgrade Metropolitanate became the seat of the Serbian church, schools and lyceums were opened, the level of literacy grew, and feudal forms of landowning gradually disappeared. The brightest pupils, mostly, but not exclusively, male, were sent to Western Europe to study – among them Nikola Pašić, who studied in Zurich in the 1870s. Many Serbs from the Habsburg Monarchy emigrated to Serbia, bringing with them a different culture and different values. The increased level of literacy and modernisation also led to the birth of nationalism. Serbs may have been Orthodox and considered traditionally pro-Russian, but German Romanticism and French revolutionary ideals were the forces that decisively shaped their nationalism.

Vuk Stefanović Karadžić reformed the language and created a simplified Cyrillic alphabet. His collections of oral poetry and writings on Serbian history, tradition and culture brought him pan-European recognition. Karadžić's nationalism was liberal by standards of the day, and he inevitably clashed with the Orthodox Church. His understanding of Serb national identity was based on language, not religion: in other words, according to Karadžić, all those who spoke Serbian were Serbs, regardless of whether they were Orthodox, Roman Catholic or Muslim.

Miloš Obrenović was acknowledged as a hereditary prince of Serbia, establishing the first modern dynasty in the country, but it was Karadjordje's son Alexander who reigned between 1842 and 1858, when the first liberal political groups emerged. Miloš had been forced to resign by liberal proto-political parties. Throughout the long 19th century the Obrenović and Karadjordjević dynasties would struggle for supremacy in Serbia, until the last Obrenović ruler, King Alexander, was murdered in a military coup in 1903. Sometimes the Petrović dynasty of Montenegro would compete with them for leadership of the Serbs. More importantly, and in addition to the dynastic rivalries, Serbia's 19th century would be dominated by a power struggle between politicians and monarchs, which led to the slow and painful birth of democratic institutions. The first modern political party was the People's Radical Party, founded in 1881 by Pašić, three years after Serbia had secured full independence from the Ottoman Empire at the Congress of Berlin.

Early years

Nikola Pašić was born on or around 19 December 1845 in Zaječar, in eastern Serbia, into a relatively poor family of merchants and farmers.[2] Arguably the greatest political leader of modern Serbia, there is some controversy over his ethnic origins, since his ancestors had migrated from present-day Macedonia. His relatively poor command of Serbian contributed to these rumours. Pašić's grammar was imperfect, he spoke slowly and quietly and was generally not a great public speaker. However, he was familiar with several languages: apart from Serbian, he spoke German and French, and had knowledge of Bulgarian and probably Russian. In any event, he had a strong sense of Serbian identity, which he maintained even during the 'Yugoslav years'.

In 1866 Pašić began studying for a degree at Belgrade's Technical Faculty. An excellent student, he won a scholarship two years later to continue his studies at the renowned Federal Polytechnic Institute in Zurich (today the Swiss Federal Institute of Technology), where he graduated as a civil engineer in 1873. Much more significant for his future career than gaining his degree was his acquaintance with Svetozar Marković – also

Zaječar-born – and a group of Serbian students influenced by the political ideas of the Russian socialists Mikhail Bakunin and Nikolai Chernyshevsky. Marković, a year younger than Pašić, died in 1875, aged just twenty-nine, and is today considered the first socialist thinker in the region. Pašić was among Marković's main followers, but whereas the latter was a theoretician, the former would prove to be above all a man of action. One of his biographers argued that Pašić's qualities as a leader were most obvious during times of crises and wars and considered him essentially a prototype Balkan revolutionary.[3]

Slightly older than other students in Zurich and an excellent, hard-working student, Pašić quickly gained the respect of his peers. Indeed, throughout his life he would be respected by others, friends and enemies alike. When the People's Radical Party was formed in 1881 there was no real leadership contest – Pašić was seen as the natural choice for party leader. He knew how to delegate and would be increasingly involved in foreign affairs, leaving domestic politics and the economy to his able aides. (While in office as Prime Minister, Pašić would usually serve as Foreign Minister.) Pašić was a pragmatist and a realist, who understood that in politics compromises have to be made. His motto was *do ut des* (a Latin saying, 'I give, so that you may give', similar in meaning to *quid pro quo*). Pašić showed no emotion in politics, whether he was dealing with an ally or an opponent. In later years he came to resemble a mystic, largely because of his long beard, relatively tall stature (at around 5 feet 7 inches [1.7m], Pašić was considered to be between medium and tall height) and calm manner. Combined with his private life, hard-working habits and natural talent for leadership, this differentiated him from his peers and may explain his extraordinary success.[4]

Pašić was never to pursue a career in civil engineering

seriously, as politics became his real passion. His other passion was history and ethnography, especially of the Balkans and Russia. He worked briefly for the Ministry for Public Works and was involved in the building of a major railway line. However, Pašić lost his civil service job because of his political activism in opposition to the government. Following his dismissal, he was involved in editing a political newspaper, but it was during the Eastern Crisis of 1875–8 that his views on the Serbian question took shape more clearly. Pašić's ideology was a mix of socialism and Serbian nationalism. His pro-Russian sentiments had less to do with his early admiration of Bakunin and Chernyshevsky than with his belief that an alliance with Russia was essential for the fulfillment of Serbia's national goals.

The first of these, shared by most 19th-century Serbian statesmen, was the struggle for full independence from the Ottoman Empire. That goal was achieved in 1878, the year Pašić, now thirty-three, was elected to parliament for the first time. The second objective was the liberation of Serbs living under foreign rule. Most Serbs from outside the Serbian principality (kingdom after 1882) lived in Bosnia-Herzegovina, which was under Austro-Hungarian military occupation and administration under the terms of the Congress of Berlin; in southern Hungary (present-day Vojvodina, northern Serbia); and in Croatia, then part of the Austro-Hungarian Empire. 'Historic' Serbian territories in the Ottoman Empire – 'Old Serbia' (Sandžak and Kosovo) and 'South Serbia' (Macedonia) – no longer had a Serb majority; the population was made up of Albanians, Macedonian Slavs and Serbian-speaking Muslims, along with Orthodox Serbs. Because the Ottoman Empire was weaker than the Habsburg Monarchy, Serbian expansion would initially take the southern route.

The Radical Party and the conflict with the Obrenović dynasty

In domestic politics, two political groups dominated Serbia when Pašić returned from Zurich – the Liberals and the Progressives – while the country was ruled by the Obrenović dynasty. Pašić's Radicals began to emerge as a new political force that successfully combined a struggle for social justice with nationalism. Such a programme appealed to the majority peasant population, who increasingly voted for the Radicals. In 1881, three years after being elected to parliament, Pašić became the leader of the newly formed People's Radical Party. He would remain at the helm of the party until his death 45 years later, spending more time as Prime Minister of Serbia and Yugoslavia than any other politician. Pašić experienced many lows as well, but he proved a master in political comeback.

In 1883 came a major survival test for the party and its leader: a peasant rebellion in the Timok region of eastern Serbia. There were several reasons for the outbreak of the rebellion. King Milan (Obrenović) refused to entrust the government to the Radicals, despite their victory in the general elections of September that year. Instead, Jovan Ristić, leader of the pro-Obrenović Liberals, was asked to form a government. This decision caused widespread dissatisfaction, especially in eastern Serbia, the Radicals' stronghold.

It was the government's decision to confiscate weapons from the population as part of military reforms which led to the rebellion. Peasants of the Timok region refused to give up their rifles, and clashes with the army followed. The rebellion was violently suppressed and the King blamed the Radicals – and Pašić in particular – for instigating it. Although the Radicals did indeed encourage the peasants' revolt, they tried to distance themselves from it once the situation got out of control. Nevertheless, the authorities ordered the arrest of the Radical leadership. Pašić and one of his closest party allies, Aca Stanojević, fled to Bulgaria. They would remain in exile for six years. The regime sentenced 94 people who had taken part in the revolt to death, including Pašić, who was sentenced *in absentia*.

During his Bulgarian exile, Pašić increasingly became interested in Macedonia and 'Old Serbia'. He believed that national liberation should be carried out in two stages: first, the 'Serbian lands' in the Ottoman Empire should be liberated, possibly in alliance with Montenegro and Bulgaria; second, the liberation of Serb-populated territories in

> **The Austrian occupation of Bosnia-Herzegovina presents less of a threat to the Serbian interests than Bulgarian [nationalist] propaganda in Macedonia and Old Serbia.**
> **NIKOLA PAŠIĆ, 1887[5]**

Austria-Hungary should follow, which could only be achieved with the aid of Russia. These ideas, developed in the 1880s, would be fulfilled two decades later: the Balkan Wars would effectively be stage one, while the First World War would present an opportunity for stage two – except that events would turn out differently, and a Yugoslav state, rather than a large Serbian one, would emerge in 1918.

Pašić's chief concern was pan-Serb liberation, but during this period he also considered the relationship between Serbs and Croats. Between 1889 and 1891 he wrote a study – published only in 1995 – entitled *Unity of Serbo-Croats*. In it, he argued that their unity was inevitable, partly because they lived intermingled. Serb-Croat unity was also desirable, since, in Pašić's view, the following century would be a *century of large and strong states* [...] *small states would not be able to survive a tough economic, political and cultural competition.*[6]

He believed that Serbs were better suited to take a leading role in the struggle for Serb-Croat unification, due to their emancipation from the Ottoman Empire, their size and their geostrategic position. The use of the term 'Serbo-Croats' suggests that Pašić believed Serbs and Croats formed a single ethnic group.

> The main dispute between Serbs and Croats is about leadership – which [group] will lead the process of bringing together Serb and Croat lands and whose tradition will prevail during the unification of Serbo-Croats.
>
> NIKOLA PAŠIĆ, C. 1889–91[7]

Return from exile

Pašić and Stanojević were pardoned by King Milan in 1889, a year after he had granted a liberal constitution – conceding to the demands of the political parties, including the Radicals. The following year Pašić married Djurdjina Duković, daughter of a rich Serb trader from Trieste. Almost completely dedicated to politics, Pašić married late in life, after his friends advised him to settle down. The Pašićes would have one son and two daughters. Pašić was a devoted husband and father who preferred to spend his evenings at home with his family. He had a soft spot for his erratic son Radomir, and stood by him even when he became involved in financial scandals. Pašić personally continued to live relatively modestly, despite marrying a rich woman.

Pašić was not only settled down and back in the country, but seemingly back in favour with the authorities. After spells as President of Parliament and Mayor of Belgrade, he was appointed Prime Minister in 1891, a post he would occupy for a year and a half. This was the first of many stints as Premier. He would be in charge of Serbian and Yugoslav governments for most of the time between 1904, when the Karadjordjevićs returned to the throne, and 1926, months before his death in December, allegedly after a bitter row with King Alexander (Karadjordjević), during which a financial scandal involving Pašić's son may have been discussed. In 1893, Pašić also served briefly as Serbia's minister to Russia.

Pašić and the Radicals seemed to have got rid of King Milan when he abdicated in favour of his minor son Alexander (Obrenović) in 1899 and went to Paris. Pašić agreed to financially support Milan's lavish lifestyle, often with Russian help, in order to keep the 'old' King outside the country. Milan, on the other hand, knew that he could blackmail Pašić: if he returned he could pose a real threat to the Radicals simply by being present in the country, where he still had considerable influence, especially in the army. Pašić also forced Milan's estranged wife, Queen Natalija, out of the country, but the King returned from exile following young King Alexander's *coup d'état* of 1893, and was appointed Chief-of-Staff of the army by his son. Pašić now faced two powerful enemies: Alexander and Milan.

In 1898 Pašić was arrested for his criticism of King Alexander. Charges of a conspiracy against the King's life were added and the Radical leader faced a death sentence for the second time in his life. He was saved by intervention from Russia, while Austria-Hungary also did not wish to see him executed. Unaware of the powerful international lobbying, Pašić agreed in prison to accept all the charges against him publicly at a show trial in exchange for an amnesty. This alienated his party colleagues – though never to the degree where they would not tolerate his presence in the party – while the public, including the peasantry, turned against their former hero as well. As the new century began, it seemed as if Pašić's political career was over.

The party also experienced its first split. In 1901 younger members of the Radical Party, long disillusioned with the party's lack of radicalism, broke away to form the Independent Radical Party – the so-called Independents. They were led by Ljubomir Davidović, future leader of the Democratic Party and Prime Minister of the Kingdom of Serbs, Croats and Slovenes in the early 1920s.

National struggle

King Alexander and Queen Draga were murdered in the early hours of 11 June (29 May OS) 1903 by a group of army officers dissatisfied with their autocratic rule and pro-Austro-Hungarian foreign policy. Despite international condemnation of the regicide – for example, Britain and the Netherlands refused to re-establish diplomatic relations with Belgrade for three years – Serbia would progress politically and economically. Democratic conditions improved, although the military continued to play a prominent role in politics. Two regional crises probably contributed to this: firstly, Austria-Hungary imposed economic sanctions on Serbia in 1906 in the so-called 'Customs War' (also known as the 'Pig War', because of Serbia's chief export to its neighbour). The embargo, introduced in order to stifle Serbia's cooperation with Bulgaria, ended in 1911, with Serbia emerging as the victor. Even more serious was the second crisis, caused by Vienna's decision to annex Bosnia-Herzegovina in 1908, which nearly led to war between Serbia and Austria-Hungary.

At the time, Pašić officially advocated the doctrine of 'The Balkans to the Balkan peoples': no foreign powers should control the Balkans and the Balkan nations should live in their own nation-states. He was mostly concerned with the idea of Serb liberation and unification, but he was also aware of the growing support for a Yugoslav unification, in the South Slav lands of Austria-Hungary and in his own Serbia. During the Balkan Wars of 1912–13, Serbia, under Pašić's leadership, would double its territory and greatly enhance its prestige among Serbs and other South Slavs living in the Habsburg Monarchy. An alliance of four Balkan states – Bulgaria, Greece, Montenegro and Serbia – declared war on the Ottoman Empire in October 1912. Within months nearly five centuries of Ottoman presence in Europe all but ended with the Treaty of London of May 1913. However, an inability to agree on the spoils of Macedonia between Bulgaria on one side and Serbia and Greece on the other led to the outbreak of the Second Balkan War in June 1913. This time everyone joined forces against Bulgaria, including Romania and the Ottoman Empire. The Bulgarians were comprehensively defeated and lost territory in Macedonia to Serbia and Greece, as well as Edirne and Thrace to Turkey; Romania, too, gained additional territory at the expense of Bulgaria, while Serbia's staunchest ally, Montenegro, also came out of the Balkan Wars with significantly more territory.

Austria-Hungary did not view Serbia's emergence as a regional power favourably, and tensions between the two countries remained high. Following the Balkan Wars, Pašić asked the leaders of the Croat-Serb Coalition (among whom was Ante Trumbić), a majority group in the Croatian *sabor* (Diet), to avoid provoking the Dual Monarchy, since Serbia was not ready for another war. He also added that [o]*ur question of liberation and unity will not be solved by the politicians of the Serb-Croat* [sic] *Coalition, but by Serbia and Russia. [However,] neither [state] is ready for war.*[8]

The assassination in Sarajevo set in motion a course of events that would eventually bring about the liberation and unification of the South Slavs; without Russia after 1917, but with the help of Britain, France and the United States. Pašić would also be wrong about the politicians of the Croat-Serb Coalition. They too would play a major role in the process of unification, perhaps none more so than Trumbić.

Pašić's position as regards Yugoslav unity has long been a matter of debate among scholars. While some have argued that he was never anything other than a Greater Serb in (poor) disguise, others have regarded him as the main architect of Yugoslavia. Pašić knew relatively little about Croatia and Slovenia – despite his wife being from Istria – and was generally mistrustful of Catholic Slavs. His interests were in the history and geography of Serbia, Montenegro, Bulgaria and Macedonia – so much so that he personally drafted some memoranda related to the eastern borders during the Paris Peace Conference. Yet, his wartime government unquestionably worked towards a South Slav union, even if Pašić did not seem to be able to distinguish between a Yugoslavia and an extended Serbia. In some ways, he was caught between the 19th-century ideals of a Serbian struggle for liberation and unification and the reality of the new, Yugoslav century that was being born.

3
Trumbić and Croatia

The emergence of modern Croatian nationalism was closely linked with the origins of the Yugoslav idea.[1] Yugoslavism was a national ideology initially based on the premise that Croats and Serbs were ethnically one nation. Eventually the Slovenes would also be considered by proponents of this ideology as members of the Yugoslav nation, but Bulgaria's separate development as a nation-state and its conflicting relationship with Serbia would ensure that the easternmost South Slav nation would usually remain outside the scope of various Yugoslav projects.

At the beginning of the 19th century historic Croatia was in a markedly different predicament from Serbia. While the Serbs' emancipation from the Ottoman Empire was gathering pace, Croatia was part of the Habsburg Monarchy, and many Croats lived in Ottoman Bosnia-Herzegovina. The Croats were even more fragmented than the Serbs. Although the old triune kingdom of Croatia-Slavonia and Dalmatia was part of the Habsburg Monarchy, it was not under one administration: Croatia (Zagreb and surrounding areas) and Slavonia were run by Budapest, while Trumbić's native Dalmatia was governed by Vienna. In addition, the Croats spoke three distinct dialects. There were no clear-cut lines between the dialects, and these in any case did not coincide with the administrative borders of the Croat provinces. Roughly speaking, Croats living in Zagreb and the Zagorje region spoke the *kajkavski* dialect, Slavonians and most Dalmatians spoke *štokavski*, while Croats from Istria and some parts of Dalmatia spoke *čakavski*. The dialects were named after different words for 'what' – *kaj*, *što*, and *ča* . There was a written literature in all three dialects. While *kajkavski* was spoken in the Croat heartland around Zagreb and in areas bordering Slovene-populated lands, there was a rich literary tradition in *štokavski* (especially in the historic city-state of Dubrovnik). Crucially, the Serbs spoke *štokavski*, as did the inhabitants of Bosnia-Herzegovina, regardless of their religion.

The 19th century was an era when intellectuals played a role as important as statesmen in creating nations, especially the small nations of East-Central Europe. Influenced by the German Romantic School, men of letters understood nations as organic wholes, as human beings. Central to national identity was language, not religion, as Vuk Karadžić demonstrated in the case of Serbia. Feeling threatened by Hungarian nationalism, a group of (*kajkavski*-speaking) Croat intellectuals, led by Ljudevit Gaj, began to emphasise linguistic similarities between Croats and Serbs and to argue that because they shared a language they belonged to a single nation. By the early 1830s Gaj and his followers had started a proto-Yugoslav movement, known as the Illyrian Movement (after the ancient people who lived in the Balkans prior to the Roman conquest). The 'Illyrians' gave up *kajkavski* and promoted *štokavski*, in order to bring Croats and Serbs closer together. They also embraced Karadžić's linguistic reforms.

At a meeting in Vienna held in March 1850 the foundations of the Serbo-Croat language were laid. The meeting was attended by eight leading linguists and literati; four Croats, three Serbs (one of them Karadžić) and one Slovene.

The Illyrian Movement grew into the Illyrian Party (later renamed the National Party), but was effectively finished by 1848. Initially supported by Vienna because of their opposition to Budapest, the Illyrians succeeded in raising awareness among the Croat masses about their Croat identity. However, the 'Yugoslav' programme largely failed, partly because of opposition from the authorities, and partly because Serbia was preoccupied with its own struggle for independence from the Ottoman Empire.

The Yugoslav programme among Croats was revived in the 1860s, this time under the leadership of Bishop Josip Juraj Strossmayer and another Catholic cleric, the historian Canon Franjo Rački. In 1867 they founded the Yugoslav Academy of Sciences and Arts in Zagreb (today, and between 1941 and 1945, called the Croatian Academy of Sciences and Arts). However, the decade also saw the emergence of the Croatian Party of Rights – 'rights' to a 'state', preserved in various legal documents and institutions such as the *sabor* (Diet) and the *ban* (governor). The founder of the party was Ante Starčević, who in his youth had supported the Illyrians. Disillusioned after the failure of Illyrianism, for which he blamed the Serbs, Starčević developed a purely Croat ideology which became extremely anti-Serb. Starčević and the Rightists regarded Serbs as 'Orthodox Croats', when they did not actually consider them an inferior 'race', and Slovenes as 'mountain' or 'Alpine' Croats; Bulgarians alone among the South Slavs were considered to be separate from Croats.

Ironically, Starčević's pan-Croat ideology would not have

been possible without obvious similarities between Serbs and Croats and other South Slavs. To a degree, a parallel may be made with Karadžić's argument that all *štokavski* speakers were Serbs. In that respect, Yugoslav, Croat and Serb nationalists all shared a belief that the South Slavs belonged to one nation, though they differed in their ideology and terminology. It was during this decade, when Croat politics was split between the followers of Starčević, Strossmayer and pro-Hungarianists, that Ante Trumbić was born.

Early years

Anton Paško (Antonio Pasquale, in the Italian version of his Christian name) Trumbić was born in Split, the largest Dalmatian town, on 17 May 1864. His parents were of peasant origins and lived in Lučac, a poor suburb of Split. The surname – originally spelled Trnbić or Tarnbich – suggests that the family originated from outside Dalmatia, and they were known as *vlaji* ('Vlachs' – a derogatory term used in Dalmatia for anyone who is not Dalmatian, and more widely in Croatia for Serbs, though there is no indication that Trumbić had Serbian, or indeed Vlach, origins).[2] Like Pašić, Trumbić's family origins are not really known.

Also like Pašić, young Anton – or Ante, as he became known – stood out for his intelligence. He was the only child in his family who went to school, and the first person from Lučac to gain a university degree. Trumbić finished secondary school in 1882 with excellent marks, although the language of instruction was not his mother tongue but Italian – secondary education in Croatian only started in Dalmatia the year after Trumbić finished school. Most young Dalmatian Croats studied at Italian universities, but Trumbić opted for Zagreb University, where he read Law. While studying in the Croat capital, he became influenced by the ideas of Starčević's Party of Rights. Having completed two years of study at Zagreb, Trumbić continued his studies in Vienna and Graz, where he graduated in 1890 and was awarded a doctorate, as was customary in Austria at the time. Trumbić – unlike Pašić – was an excellent linguist, fluent in Italian, German and French.

Even before completing his degree, Trumbić started working as a lawyer in his native Split and in Trogir, a nearby town. In 1888 he was forced to interrupt practising as a judge because of his support for two local Serb politicians accused of anti-Habsburg activities. Eventually, in 1894, aged thirty, he passed the solicitor's examination and opened a legal practice in Split. The same year he joined the Croatian Party of Rights for Dalmatia. Just over a decade later, in 1905, he would become Mayor of Split.

Devoted to politics and the legal profession, Trumbić had little time for private life. When he was elected a deputy in the *Reichsrat* (Austrian parliament) in 1897, his friend and political ally Frano Supilo jokingly advised him to use his new political influence and wealth to attract a young wife. However, like Pašić, Trumbić would marry only in his forties. On 10 February 1906, aged 42, he married Ana Karaman, sister of a well-known Croatian art historian and archaeologist. 'When will the Lord Mayor of Split get an heir?', Supilo asked teasingly in September that year. The answer would be never, as the Trumbićes would have no children.[3]

Frano Supilo (1870–1917) was one of Trumbić's closest political allies until they fell out in 1916. Born in Cavtat, Dalmatia, Supilo was a member of the Party of Rights, and one of the creators of the Rijeka Resolution and the 'New Course'. He was among the leading members of the Croat-Serb Coalition and, between 1914 and 1916, one of the two leaders of the Yugoslav Committee (Trumbić was the other one). Supilo died in London.

Life in Politics

At the time of Trumbić's birth, the Austrian Empire was going through a profound political crisis, caused both by external and internal factors. In 1866 Austria fought and lost a war against Prussia, which led to the former leaving the German Confederation (created at the 1815 Congress of Vienna, which replaced the Holy Roman Empire, abolished by Napoleon in 1806). Internally, the Empire was particularly destabilised by Hungarian nationalism. In 1867 Vienna and Budapest reached a Compromise (*Ausgleich*) which turned the Habsburg dominions into the Dual Monarchy. This essentially meant power-sharing between the Germans/Austrians and Hungarians, as reflected in the new name for the state: Austria-Hungary. The Austrian Emperor was the King of Hungary, and there were two governments, one in Vienna and one in Budapest. The *Ausgleich* made the administrative divisions of the South Slav and 'Croatian' lands more firmly set.

If Hungarian nationalism arguably posed the greatest challenge to the government in Vienna, it was not the only nationalism which threatened the Empire's unity. Nor were the Austrians the sole target of the Empire's nationalities. The Kingdom of Hungary, incorporated into Austria in 1526, was an empire within an empire, incorporating numerous historic kingdoms and provinces and a large number of national minorities, including Croats, Slovaks, Romanians and Serbs. The Croats in particular took advantage of the 1867 Compromise to secure their own agreement with Hungary, which in 1868 granted Croatia-Slavonia more autonomy within the Kingdom of Hungary. This event is known as the Hungarian-Croatian Compromise (*nagodba*). However, the Croats, like other nationalities, continued to aspire to greater autonomy, if not outright independence.

Although there were pro-Hungarian Croatian politicians, the so-called 'Magyarones', there was a strong Croat nationalist movement which fought against what it perceived as the hegemony of Budapest. Autonomous Croatia did not enjoy much financial autonomy. Furthermore, it was exposed to a Hungarian cultural and political domination that threatened eventually to assimilate non-Hungarians.

In 1883 Budapest appointed Károly Khuen-Héderváry as *ban* (governor) of Croatia. During his twenty-year period in office, he curbed calls for greater autonomy for Croatia and pursued policies of magyarization. For instance, Hungarian was made the official language. In a classic example of 'divide and rule', Khuen-Héderváry secured support among some Serbs who lived in Croatia, leading to increased anti-Serb sentiment among many Croats. Khuen-Héderváry's governorship is generally perceived to have had a negative impact on Croat-Serb relations.

At the time when Trumbić entered politics, political life in Croatia was split into two main factions: supporters and opponents of the 1868 Compromise. The latter were further divided into two main groups: followers of Bishop Strossmayer and followers of Ante Starčević, or, in other words, those who favoured cooperation with the Serbs and advocated Yugoslavist ideals, and those who were chiefly Croat nationalists, some of whom were also anti-Serb.

When Trumbić joined Starčević's Party of Rights in 1894, the party was itself divided between moderates, who were in favour of cooperation with Serbs, and hard-line nationalists. The latter broke away under the leadership of Josip Frank, who formed the Pure Party of Rights (also known as the Frankists), but Trumbić remained in the moderate faction, which, according to some historians, received Starčević's support shortly before his death in 1896. Trumbić was not fully satisfied with the party programme, which he considered to be too theoretical. A young, energetic man from the sunny Dalmatian coast, he craved political action – another parallel with Pašić. Trumbić and Supilo initiated a unification of various regional branches of the party. Having been elected to the Dalmatian provincial *sabor* soon after joining the party, Trumbić was then appointed to the Vienna *Reichsrat*.

> A Croat in Dalmatia, in Zagreb, in Istria, everywhere, must have one aim, one aspiration – the emancipation of the Croat nation.
>
> ANTE TRUMBIĆ, 1887[4]

Trumbić advocated the administrative unification of Dalmatia with Croatia-Slavonia. Zagreb was, in his view, the centre around which all Croat lands should unify. The Croats had tried but failed to bring together the historic provinces under the terms of the Croat-Hungarian Compromise. The chief obstacle was Vienna, which did not want to see more territory transferred to Hungary's control.

Trumbić was among the main authors of a declaration of March 1897, which proclaimed Dalmatia to be a Croat land and demanded its unification with Croatia-Slavonia. The resolution was presented to the *Reichsrat*, but was swiftly rejected. Not until the creation of the Kingdom of Serbs, Croats and Slovenes would all Croat lands come under a single administration. Although many in Croatia would later feel alienated by a centralist regime in Belgrade, the support for Yugoslavia among Croats in 1918 was partly due to their desire to unify all their 'historic lands' in one state. That was certainly the case with Trumbić, who during the war was among the leading proponents of a united Yugoslavia. A similar goal – to see all, or at least most of, their compatriots and historic lands united in one state – was the reason why Pašić and the Serbs of various political backgrounds supported the creation of Yugoslavia in 1918.

The 'New Course'

In the early 20th century, Trumbić's ideology would increasingly shift towards Yugoslavism. He would, in fact, work towards bringing together the two main strands of Croatian politics of the second half of the 19th century: the pan-Yugoslav one of Bishop Strossmayer and the pan-Croat one of Ante Starčević. Trumbić was among the initiators in April 1905 of the unification of the Party of Rights and the People's Party (the pan-Yugoslav party, of Gaj and later Strossmayer, that was originally called the Illyrian Party), into the new, Croatian Party. This would be a turning-point in the development of Trumbić's national ideology.

Soon after its formation, the Croatian Party proclaimed that its programme was based on two main principles: firstly, that the Kingdom of Dalmatia should be united with the Kingdom of Croatia-Slavonia, on the basis of national as well as state rights; and, secondly, that the Party regarded Croats and Serbs as members of one nation, 'according to their blood and their language', and inseparable geographically. The Croatian Party pledged to work towards resolving old conflicts between Serbs and Croats. This programme paved the way for the 'New Course' – a closer cooperation between major Croat, Serb, Hungarian and Italian parties in opposition to Vienna.

Trumbić's newly-found Yugoslavism was both sincere and pragmatic. Like many Croats at the time, he believed that Austria posed the greatest threat to Croat national aspirations. Hungarians could not be relied upon as allies because of their own nationalism, which threatened Croats and their identity. Therefore, he believed that Croats should work closely with Serbs and Italians. This was ironic, since the zenith of his political career – the Paris Peace Conference – would be marked by a political struggle against Italian aspirations in Istria, Fiume and Dalmatia, and would further destabilise his relationship with Pašić, who in turn was more willing to reach a compromise with Italy.

It may be argued that Trumbić's Yugoslavism developed gradually, and that in the late 19th and early 20th century he was more of a pragmatist than a genuine believer in Yugoslav unity. For example, in 1897 he publicly rejected the Yugoslav idea, claiming that it was *detested* and *finished* among Croats. However, at the same time he called for a reconciliation and close cooperation between Croats and Serbs. Supilo, on the other hand, appeared more supportive of Yugoslavism at this time, stating that 'Croats and Serbs were completely one nation with two equal names'.[5]

In any event, the politics of the New Course brought together the main Croatian and Serbian political parties. In October 1905, Croatian parties met in Fiume (Rijeka) and issued the so-called Rijeka Resolution, supporting the Hungarian struggle for self-determination and demanding the same right for other nationalities in the Empire, including the Croats. The Croatian deputies also demanded the establishment of democratic institutions, free speech, freedom of the press and of assembly, and independent courts. Soon afterwards their Serb counterparts convened in Zara (Zadar), issuing the so-called Zadar Resolution, which supported the demands of the Rijeka Resolution.

The Croat-Serb Coalition was formed soon afterwards. It won elections for the *sabor* in May 1906, becoming the dominant force in Croatian politics over the following decade or so. Just as the threat of Magyarisation had encouraged the formation of the Illyrian Movement in the 1830s, so the perceived threat of German/Austrian nationalism brought together Habsburg Croats and Serbs in the early 20th century. Unlike the Illyrian Movement, however, which, initially at least, was cultural, the Croat-Serb Coalition was above all a political movement. If the Illyrians' proto-Yugoslavism was the first phase in the development of the Yugoslav Idea, Strossmayer's Yugoslavism the second, the Yugoslavism of the Coalition was the third. The 'national oneness' ideology of the Croat-Serb Coalition was based on the notion that Croats and Serbs were a single nation that should enjoy the right to self-determination. The increasing popularity of the Coalition was at the expense of Frank's party and pro-Hungarian Croat politicians.

> Croats and Serbs are a single national being. They live and will live under one roof.
>
> **ANTE TRUMBIĆ, 1905**[6]

Following the emergence of the Croat-Serb Coalition, events elsewhere in the region began to move in favour of the formation of a Yugoslavia. While the creation of a united, large South Slav state was by no means inevitable, certainly not until the late stages of the First World War, in retrospect it may be argued that the crisis over the annexation of Bosnia-Herzegovina by Austria-Hungary in 1908 and the Balkan Wars of 1912–13 created an atmosphere that was favourable to Yugoslav nationalism. The first event nearly led to a war between the Dual Monarchy and Serbia, where after 1903 and the assassination of the last Obrenović king, foreign policy had become more pro-Russian and anti-Habsburg. Within Austria-Hungary, Serbs and other South Slavs increasingly looked towards Serbia and away from Budapest and Vienna. Serbia's prestige – at least among many Habsburg South Slavs, including Trumbić – increased as much as its territory had following its victories in the two Balkan Wars. It seemed as if a confrontation between the expanding, aggressive little kingdom and the large but internally divided Empire would happen sooner or later, though few expected it to happen so soon after the Balkan Wars. Not many could have predicted either that this confrontation would trigger a global conflict, the first of the 20th century.

On the eve of the First World War, Trumbić and his Dalmatian colleagues Supilo and Josip Smodlaka concentrated their efforts in working towards independence for the Habsburg South Slavs and their unification with Serbia and Montenegro. In late 1913 Trumbić and Smodlaka met with two Bosnian Serb politicians and discussed joint political action that would aim to unite all Yugoslavs into one state. They agreed that in the event of war they would emigrate and campaign for the unification with Serbia from abroad. But even they were surprised at how soon they would be presented with an opportunity to do exactly that.

Following the Sarajevo assassination on 28 June 1914 and before Austria-Hungary's declaration of war on Serbia exactly one month later, Trumbić moved to Italy. From Rome, together with Supilo and the internationally-renowned sculptor Ivan Meštrović, he campaigned for a Yugoslav unification. At the same time, they began to lobby the governments of France, Britain and Russia against Italy's claims to Dalmatia. This was the beginning of a four-year propaganda struggle carried out by the Yugoslav Committee, led by Trumbić and Supilo, and, from 1915, based in London.

4

War and Unification

Soon after the First World War broke out, with Austria-Hungary's attack on Serbia on 28 July 1914, the Pašić government laid out its war aims. In early September 1914, Pašić informed Serbia's representatives in Allied countries that *our aim is to create, out of Serbia, a powerful south-western Slav state, that would include all Serbs, all Croats and all Slovenes.*[1] On 7 December, the government, evacuated to the southern city of Niš, formally proclaimed its aim to 'liberate and unite all our unliberated brethren: Serbs, Croats, and Slovenes' into one state.[2] Trumbić had in the meantime gone into exile, first to Italy then to London, whence he would run the Yugoslav Committee of pro-Yugoslav émigrés from Austria-Hungary. In addition to Trumbić and Supilo, the Committee members included such prominent South Slavs as the sculptor Meštrović. Most members of the Committee were Croats, but there were also Serbs and Slovenes. The Pašić government supported the Committee financially. However, Trumbić and Supilo refused to accept money from the government for their personal needs, in order to maintain their political independence. The Committee also enjoyed support

Europe 1914

Petrograd (St Petersburg)

○Riga

○Moscow

○Vilna

Königsberg

nzig

RUSSIAN EMPIRE

Warsaw ○Brest-Litovsk

Kiev○

○Budapest

'GARY

Odessa

ROMANIA

Belgrade Bucharest○

Black Sea

SERBIA **BULGARIA**

EGRO ○Sofia

ana○

LBANIA

Constantinople

GREECE

OTTOMAN EMPIRE

○Athens

among prominent British public figures, including the academic RW Seton-Watson and the journalist Henry Wickham Steed.

Three wartime events decisively shaped the relationship between Pašić and Trumbić and would have a major impact on the future Yugoslav union. First, the secret Treaty of London of April 1915, which offered Italy most of the eastern Adriatic in exchange for entering the war on the Allied side; the Treaty was kept secret from Serbia. Second, the negotiations between the Serbian government and the Yugoslav Committee at Corfu in summer 1917. Third, the Geneva talks of November 1918 between the main political leaders from Serbia and the Habsburg Yugoslav provinces. At Corfu and in Geneva, the two concepts of Yugoslavia represented by Pašić and Trumbić would clash, but neither came out as a clear winner. The two visions would continue to compete during the Peace Conference in Paris and in its aftermath.

The Treaty of London

Christmas 1914 had come and gone, but the end of the war was nowhere in sight. The belligerent parties, once confident the war would be over by the year's end, began to negotiate with the one major European power that was still neutral – Italy – hoping that Rome would tip the balance in their favour. Despite being a member of the pre-war Triple Alliance with Austria-Hungary and Germany, Italy was not bound to join the war. The Italians also aspired to territories controlled by the Central Powers – specifically the Habsburg-held eastern Adriatic. Negotiations between Italy, Britain, France and Russia began in March 1915. By the end of May, Italy had joined the war on the Allied side, by declaring war on Austria-Hungary.

The negotiations lasted for some six weeks, and were kept secret. The secrecy was partly deemed necessary because the Allies hoped to gain a considerable psychological advantage over the enemy by a surprise announcement of Italy's adherence to the Entente camp. Another reason was Serbia. For the Allies' bait to Italy was the promise of Istria and Dalmatia (but not Fiume) and control over Albania – promises necessary to win over Italy but bound to be resisted by Serbia, which regarded Dalmatia as a Yugoslav land and had its own designs *vis-à-vis* Albania. This was the reason why the Allies also promised Italy that the terms of the treaty would not be revealed to other countries, Serbia in particular.

Not that Serbia and the South Slavs were completely ignored by the Allies during the negotiations. The text of the Treaty of London, signed on 26 April 1915, but published only after the war, reveals that the four powers envisaged certain territories in Dalmatia going to 'Croatia, Serbia and Montenegro'.[3]

As was perhaps to be expected, Russia expressed the greatest concern for Serbia's interests. Britain and France were led by more pragmatic considerations: Italy could tip the balance in the Allies' favour. Should it join the Central Powers, the Allies would be in a difficult position. The Russian military saw the point and put pressure on its country's Foreign Minister, Sergei Sazonov, who finally, on 21 April, authorised Russia's ambassador to London, Count Alexander von Beckendorff, to sign the treaty.

Soon after the negotiations with Italy had started, rumours began to circulate among the South Slav leaders that the four Powers were discussing territories they regarded as rightfully theirs. Despite Serbia's status as an ally and the Habsburg South Slavs' contacts in Britain, the Yugoslavs had been unable to find out any details about the ongoing talks for several weeks. In fact, they did not know for certain how much truth there was, if any, in the rumours and whether any talks were indeed taking place.

Pašić had first learned that something was going on in mid-March from Serbia's minister to Rome, who travelled to the temporary capital in Niš to alert the Prime Minister. Pašić made enquiries with the Russians, but Petrograd remained ominously silent. His ministers to London (Mateja Bošković, who would be a member of the Yugoslav delegation in Paris) and Petrograd fared no better. Trumbić failed to get any relevant information either, despite his indirect contacts with the Foreign Office. It was Frano Supilo, at the time on a visit to Petrograd, who received the first concrete evidence of the talks from Sazonov, and who urged Pašić and Trumbić to act.

Neither Pašić nor Prince Regent Alexander of Serbia were able to persuade Russia to impede the treaty. Alexander made a personal appeal to Prince Trubetskoi, Russia's minister to Serbia, to prevent the imposition of Italian domination over the South Slavs, which in his opinion would lead to a war, just as Austrian domination had done. Independently of the Serbian Prince Regent, Trumbić issued a similar warning to the Russian minister in Rome, on 26 April – by coincidence, the very same day the treaty was signed, unbeknown to Trumbić and the Serbian government. Meanwhile, Pašić's request to travel to Russia was turned down by Sazonov. The Serbian Prime Minister cabled a message to the Russian Foreign Minister, warning that *the Southern Slavs could not enjoy friendly and close relations with Italians, except in the event of their receiving, together with liberty, their part of the Adriatic coast. United, the Serbs, Croats and Slovenes who inhabit Serbia, Montenegro, Hercegovina, Bosnia, Croatia, Slavonia, Dalmatia, Istria, Carinthia and Carniola, will constitute for Italy a powerful rampart against German assault.*[4]

The very real possibility that the Allies would promise the eastern Adriatic to Italy became the *affaire du jour* in war-ravaged Serbia. The Serbian parliament convened in Niš on 28 April to discuss the situation; the mood was one of anger and bitterness. But the Russians' minds were made up and neither the Serbs nor the Yugoslav émigrés were able to change them. Petrograd was genuinely sympathetic to the South Slavs' demands and was aware of the possible implications the concessions to Italy might have on Serbia's internal politics. However, above all, Russia's position was determined by its own interests, which, in this case, demanded that Italy be appeased and brought into the Allied camp by a promise of Istria and Dalmatia. 'Neither the Heir Apparent [Prince Regent Alexander] nor the Serbian government can doubt our ardent desire to defend Slav interests within limits of the possible', Sazonov wrote to Trubetskoi. 'If we do not find it possible to fulfil in large measure all the wishes of the Slavs, this must be attributed to special circumstances ... Our rejection of his visit can be used by Pašić for his own justification in Serbian political circles.'[5]

Contrary to expectations on all sides, Italy's entry into the war failed to bring about a quick, decisive victory for the Allies. If anything, it may be argued that it had the opposite effect; it alienated Serbia, mobilised the Yugoslav émigrés abroad and boosted the morale of South Slav soldiers in the Habsburg army, more determined than ever to fight against the Italians.

Serbia's initial reaction to its inability to influence talks with Italy was one of anger, and it issued threats to its allies.

On 4 May Pašić told the British, French and Russian ministers in Niš that his government regarded the territorial concessions to Italy as an *open question*, presumably to be discussed after the war. The same day, the Serbian parliament passed a resolution calling on the Allies to prevent the secret treaty from coming into effect. On 5 May Prince Regent Alexander wrote a letter to his great-uncle Grand Duke Nikolai Nikolaevich, protesting against the concessions Russia and its allies had made to Italy. He also warned that Serbia would send troops to Montenegro to prevent an Italian landing in southern Dalmatia.[6] Meanwhile, the Yugoslav Committee issued a Manifesto on 12 May, calling for the liberation and unification of all South Slavs, and submitted a similar memorandum to the Foreign Ministers of Great Britain, France and Russia. It also issued an appeal to the British nation and to the Westminster Parliament, which received considerable publicity, but had no real effect. Nevertheless, it may be argued that the secret Treaty of London inspired an intensive and concerted campaign by the Yugoslav Committee which would last until the end of the war.

The Serbian military reacted with a combination of passivity and action. Serbian troops went quiet on the Austrian front, but began to move towards Albania, which was practically an Italian protectorate. Sidney Sonnino, Italy's Foreign Minister, urged Britain, France and Russia to force Serbia to employ its troops more actively against Austria-Hungary and to stop advancing towards Albania. Pašić remained unmoved. 'If Serbia were allied with Austria she would not have acted differently', Sonnino stated angrily in June 1915.[7]

That summer relations between Serbia and the Allies remained tense. On 16 August, British, French and Russian ministers in Niš handed Pašić a joint declaration, based on a memorandum by the British Foreign Secretary, Sir Edward Grey, which offered Serbia a 'compensation' in Bosnia-Herzegovina, southern Hungary, Slavonia, the southern Adriatic and parts of northern Albania (to be shared with Montenegro), in exchange for giving up Macedonia. The Allies hoped to win over Bulgaria by offering it Serbian Macedonia. Pašić was bitterly disappointed, and complained to Trumbić that Serbia clearly had to struggle against its allies, as well as against its enemies. When Trubetskoi warned him that Serbia had to choose, otherwise it might end up without both Macedonia and the lands the Allies were offering, Pašić replied: *We shall choose Macedonia*. Grey and his French counterpart Théophile Delcassé both wrote to Pašić, reassuring him that should Serbia wish to unite with Croatia after the war, they would support it. When Pašić asked about Slovenia, Sazonov explained to him that by 'Croatia' the Allies meant all Habsburg South Slav territories not promised to Italy.[8]

It is sometimes suggested that during this period the Pašić government was offered a 'Greater Serbia' in order to give up its pan-Yugoslav claims in the eastern Adriatic and that the Serbian government rejected this alleged offer out of its sense of duty towards other South Slavs. In reality, the Serbs (and Montenegrins) were neither consulted nor informed about the negotiations with Italy. Moreover, the fact that Croatia, as well as Montenegro, was mentioned in the Treaty of London, suggests that the Allies did not consider only Serbia's interests among the South Slavs, despite the fact that Serbia was an ally, and Croatia part of the territory of an enemy country. Although in the summer of 1915 the Allies proposed to the Serbian government territorial compensation at the expense of the Habsburg Monarchy in exchange for Serbia giving up Macedonia, similar bargaining with territories was common during the war, and more often than not wartime promises would not be fulfilled at the Peace Conference.

It is not easy to provide a simple explanation for the main actors' motives. Serbia's coalition government preferred the creation of a large South Slav state. The Independents and Progressives were overall more genuinely Yugoslav than the Radicals. Pašić was primarily concerned with pan-Serb unification, which could only be achieved at the expense of Austria-Hungary. A large Serb state may have been Pašić's preferred outcome but, ever a realist, he realised that it was unlikely to gain enough support, externally or internally. The disintegration of Austria-Hungary would have been necessary for such an outcome, but this was not an Allied war aim until later stages of the war, if indeed even then. Russia may have preferred a large Serbia instead of an even larger, but not predominantly Orthodox, Yugoslavia. Britain, on the other hand, probably preferred a Yugoslavia to the Russian satellite in the Balkans that Greater Serbia might have turned into. The creation of Yugoslavia was the main aim of the British-based Yugoslav Committee. Pašić came to believe that Serb unification could only be achieved in collaboration with anti-Habsburg and pro-Yugoslav Croat and Slovene leaders. He also believed that large states would be better suited to withstand domination by powerful neighbours in a post-war order, and after 1917 he would lose his main ally among the Great Powers, Russia. In other words, it may be argued that during the First World War both Serbian and Croatian leaders saw Yugoslavia as the best protection from Italy and from pan-Germanism. It is debatable, in any case, whether a viable alternative to a Yugoslav state would have been available at the end of the war.[9]

Following Serbia's military defeat in late 1915, King Peter

I, the government, and a decimated army reached the safety of the Greek island of Corfu after an epic retreat through the mountains of Montenegro and Albania. Such a precarious situation allegedly led Pašić to backtrack on the issue of the creation of a Yugoslavia in 1916, but the Serbian Prince Regent Alexander continued to support Yugoslav unification publicly.

At a reception in London's Claridge's Hotel[10] in April that year, Alexander told his British hosts that the Serbian army fought for 'the ideal towards the attainment of which we have striven for centuries. This ideal is the union in one single fatherland of all the Serbs, Croats and Slovenes, who are one people with the same traditions, the same tongue, the same tendencies, but whom an evil fate has divided.'[11]

The suspicion that the Serbian government-in-exile was no longer firmly in favour of a Yugoslavia led to a conflict within the Yugoslav Committee. Supilo wanted the Committee to sever its relations with Pašić and his ministers, but Trumbić refused to take such a radical action. In this he was supported by other members of the Committee, who believed that the two sides must work together towards unification, while any differences would be worked out after the war. Supilo resigned from the Committee in protest,

Alexander Karadjordjević (1888–1934) was the second son of King Peter I of Serbia and Princess Zorka of Montenegro, who died before her husband became king in 1903. Born in Cetinje and educated in Geneva, St Petersburg and Belgrade, he became heir to the throne in 1909, because his elder brother George's temper was deemed unsuitable for a future king. In June 1914 Crown Prince Alexander was proclaimed the Regent of Serbia and thereafter ruled in the name of his ailing father. Alexander became King of Serbs, Croats and Slovenes upon the death of Peter I in August 1921. In January 1929, he proclaimed a dictatorship, and later that year renamed the country Yugoslavia. In October 1934 he was assassinated while on a state visit to France by a Macedonian revolutionary acting on behalf of Croat *Ustašas*.

effectively ending his political career even before his untimely death the following year.

The conflict between Trumbić and Supilo was not the only disagreement within the Committee. Its dependence on Serbia and the Entente, a lack of political legitimacy, and its ethnically mixed membership all created antagonisms. All these factors unquestionably weakened the Committee's position *vis-à-vis* the Serbian government and those South Slav leaders who remained in Austria-Hungary.

The Corfu Declaration

1917 proved to be a particularly eventful year. In February, a spontaneous uprising against the occupying forces broke out in the Serbian region of Toplica, only to be brutally suppressed the following month.[12] In May, the Habsburg South Slavs pushed for more autonomy within the Empire. During the spring a three-sided power struggle between Prince Regent Alexander and a group of officers loyal to him (known as the 'White Hand'), Colonel Dragutin Dmiitrijević Apis and the 'Black Hand', and Pašić's Radicals reached its peak. The 'Black Hand' officers were accused of conspiring against the government and even of plotting the assassination of the Prince Regent. Although the evidence was not conclusive, Apis and two other members of the secret organisation were executed in June, after a show trial held in Salonica. Pašić's support of the Prince Regent was tactical and led to the collapse of the coalition government; soon after the trial, he formed a purely Radical government. Pašić had once again shown his survival instincts. Although Pašić and Alexander got rid of a dangerous political opponent, they were not political allies. The whole episode in fact further damaged their relationship, and somewhat marred Serbia's international reputation.[13] In hindsight, it was an early sign of the Prince Regent's autocratic tendencies. Just over a decade later he would become the dictator of Yugoslavia.

In the international arena, the entry of the United States of America into the war in April and Russia's withdrawal following the November (October OS) Revolution resulted in two turning points. President Woodrow Wilson of the United States championed the small nations' right to self-determination – although his Fourteen Points of January 1918 did not advocate the dissolution of the Habsburg Monarchy – and opposed the policy of secret treaties (as did Vladimir Ilich Lenin, though for different ideological reasons). At the same time Pašić lost a powerful ally in Russia, which had viewed Yugoslav unification with some suspicion.

In June and July, the Serbian government and the Yugoslav Committee met for talks on Corfu. Pašić and Trumbić issued a joint declaration, announcing that after the war, Serbs, Croats and Slovenes, 'also known as South Slavs or Yugoslavs', would unite in a single state, that would be a constitutional, democratic and parliamentary monarchy under the Karadjordjević dynasty, and which would be called the Kingdom of Serbs, Croats and Slovenes. The future state was thus predestined to become a monarchy under the Serbian dynasty even before it was created, and before such vital decisions could be tested by democratic means.[14] Pašić and Trumbić failed to specify whether the Serb-Croat-Slovene state should be a centralised or a decentralised one, and are often blamed by historians for this failure.

In a debate with Pašić's Radicals in the mid-1920s, Trumbić argued that he had resolutely rejected centralism at Corfu.[15] However, he had also expressed reservations about federalism, stating during the Corfu Conference that, while in favour

PRESIDENT WILSON'S FOURTEEN POINTS, 8 JANUARY 1918

The program of the world's peace, therefore, is our program; and that program, the only possible program, as we see it, is this:

I. Open covenants of peace, openly arrived at, after which there shall be no private international understandings of any kind but diplomacy shall proceed always frankly and in the public view.

II. Absolute freedom of navigation upon the seas, outside territorial waters, alike in peace and in war, except as the seas may be closed in whole or in part by international action for the enforcement of international covenants.

III. The removal, so far as possible, of all economic barriers and the establishment of an equality of trade conditions among all the nations consenting to the peace and associating themselves for its maintenance.

IV. Adequate guarantees given and taken that national armaments will be reduced to the lowest point consistent with domestic safety.

V. A free, open-minded, and absolutely impartial adjustment of all colonial claims, based upon a strict observance of the principle that in determining all such questions of sovereignty the interests of the populations concerned must have equal weight with the equitable claims of the government whose title is to be determined.

VI. The evacuation of all Russian territory and such a settlement of all questions affecting Russia as will secure the best and freest cooperation of the other nations of the world in obtaining for her an unhampered and unembarrassed opportunity for the independent determination of her own political development and national policy and assure her of a sincere welcome into the society of free nations under institutions of her own choosing; and, more than a welcome, assistance also of every kind that she may need and may herself desire. The treatment accorded Russia by her sister nations in the months to come will be the acid test of their good will, of their comprehension of her needs as distinguished from their own interests, and of their intelligent and unselfish sympathy.

VII. Belgium, the whole world will agree, must be evacuated and restored, without any attempt to limit the sovereignty which she enjoys in common with all other free nations. No other single act will serve as this will serve to restore confidence among the nations in the laws which they have themselves set and determined for the government of their relations with one another. Without this healing act the whole structure and validity of international law is forever impaired.

VIII. All French territory should be freed and the invaded portions restored, and the wrong done to France by Prussia in 1871 in the matter of Alsace-Lorraine, which has unsettled the peace of the world for nearly fifty years, should be righted, in order that peace may once more be made secure in the interest of all.

IX. A readjustment of the frontiers of Italy should be effected along clearly recognizable lines of nationality.

X. The peoples of Austria-Hungary, whose place among the nations we wish to see safeguarded and assured, should be accorded the freest opportunity to autonomous development.

XI. Rumania, Serbia, and Montenegro should be evacuated; occupied territories restored; Serbia accorded free and secure access to the sea; and the relations of the several Balkan states to one another determined by friendly counsel along historically established lines of allegiance and nationality; and international guarantees of the political and economic independence and territorial integrity of the several Balkan states should be entered into.

XII. The Turkish portion of the present Ottoman Empire should be assured a secure sovereignty, but the other nationalities which are now under Turkish rule should be assured an undoubted security of life and an absolutely unmolested opportunity of autonomous development, and the Dardanelles should be permanently opened as a free passage to the ships and commerce of all nations under international guarantees.

XIII. An independent Polish state should be erected which should include the territories inhabited by indisputably Polish populations, which should be assured a free and secure access to the sea, and whose political and economic independence and territorial integrity should be guaranteed by international covenant.

XIV. A general association of nations must be formed under specific covenants for the purpose of affording mutual guarantees of political independence and territorial integrity to great and small states alike.

of wide regional autonomies, *I do not have any illusions in respect to a federal system of government, because I cannot see how it would benefit the progress of our national development.*[16] Although both sides formally rejected federalism, centralism was not the generally-accepted alternative. Those who, like Trumbić, opposed centralism, argued for a compromise solution, a system of government that was neither centralist nor federalist, but they did not fully elaborate what that would involve.

Trumbić was aware that a compromise with Pašić was essential if the Yugoslav movement was to achieve its ultimate aim. For Trumbić, there was no alternative to Yugoslavia. Croatia would have emerged from the war as a former enemy state within reduced borders, probably heavily dependent on its powerful Serbian neighbour, which would in all likelihood have incorporated Bosnia-Herzegovina and Serb-populated areas of Croatia, possibly including large parts of Trumbić's Dalmatia.

The Unification

During the summer of 1918, Pašić and Trumbić clashed over the question of recognition of a 'Yugoslav government in exile' by the Allies, who had just recognised the Czechoslovak and Polish émigré committees as national governments. When in July Trumbić suggested to Pašić that the Yugoslav Committee should seek similar recognition, the Serbian Prime Minister objected: *Serbia ... internationally represents our nation of three names ... It is obvious therefore that there is no need to ask the Allies to do the same thing with us which they have done with the Czecho-Slovaks and the Poles, for these two nations have not got their own free state, to represent their Piedmont.*[17]

Trumbić and the Yugoslav Committee would be under-
mined in a different way by events on the ground. On 8
October, the Habsburg Yugoslavs formed the National
Council, a *de facto* government based in Zagreb for the
South Slav lands of the disintegrating Habsburg Monarchy.
Anton Korošec, leader of the Slovene Clericals, was elected
its president, while Ante Pavelić and Svetozar Pribićević, the
leading Croat and Serb in the Croat-Serb coalition, respectively, became its vice-presidents (Pavelić is not to be confused with the *Ustaša* leader of the same name). On 29
October the National Council declared the formation of the
State of Slovenes, Croats, and Serbs. It proclaimed that 'the
Yugo-slavs were a single, indivisible people' who demanded
'national self-determination'; it promised to 'grant cultural
privileges to any racial minorities in their midst' and to open
the Adriatic ports to 'free commerce'; finally, it demanded
that the State be represented at the future peace conference.
Euphoric South Slav deputies sang the Serbian national
anthem and *La Marseillaise*. The *ban* of Croatia proclaimed
that there was no longer a need for the *sabor* to exist, as
there was no more Croatia. Public celebrations were held in
Ljubljana as well.[18]

Meanwhile, the Serbian army successfully liberated the
country, entering Belgrade on 1 November, and expelling
the last enemy troops from Serbian territory two days later.
Serbian troops now marched into the South Slav lands of
Austria-Hungary, just as Italian forces were moving into territories promised to Italy by the Treaty of London.

Representatives of the Serbian government, the main
Serbian opposition parties, the National Council and the
Yugoslav Committee met in Geneva in early November 1918
to discuss the terms of unification. The aim of the meeting

was to produce a declaration on Yugoslav unification to be presented to the Allies. Differences immediately emerged. Pašić predictably argued that Serbia was best placed to advocate the Yugoslav union and should therefore play a leading role. Representatives of the National Council argued that the State of Slovenes, Croats and Serbs should be Serbia's equal partner. They were supported by the Yugoslav Committee and by the Serbian opposition. Outnumbered, the Serbian Prime Minister reluctantly backed down. On 8 November he officially recognised the State of Slovenes, Croats and Serbs, calling on the Allies to follow his example, and the following day a joint declaration was issued.

The Geneva Declaration stipulated that the existing institutions of Serbia and of the State of Slovenes, Croats and Serbs should remain until a Constituent Assembly was formed, and envisaged a joint interim government. However, thanks to Pašić's manoeuvring, the Declaration came to nothing. The Serbian government in Corfu refused to ratify it after Pašić had falsely claimed that Prince Regent Alexander also opposed it. There were dissenting voices in Zagreb as well, where Pribićević in particular was critical of the Declaration. As a result of the ultimate failure of the Geneva talks, the relationship between Belgrade and Zagreb was tense during the weeks preceding unification.

On 1 December 1918 in Belgrade, a delegation of the National Council which had arrived in Belgrade following a long and intense debate over the terms of unification formally asked Prince Regent Alexander to declare the South Slav union. He duly obliged, proclaiming the 'unification of Serbia with the lands of the independent State of Slovenes, Croats and Serbs into the united Kingdom of Serbs, Croats and Slovenes'.[19] Neither Pašić nor Trumbić was there to witness the historic moment. Yet, events of the next few weeks would bring them together again, as two leading representatives of the Kingdom of Serbs, Croats and Slovenes at the Peace Conference in Paris.

Nikola Pašić the Prime Minister of Serbia (above)
Ante Trumbić (right)

II
The Paris Peace Conference

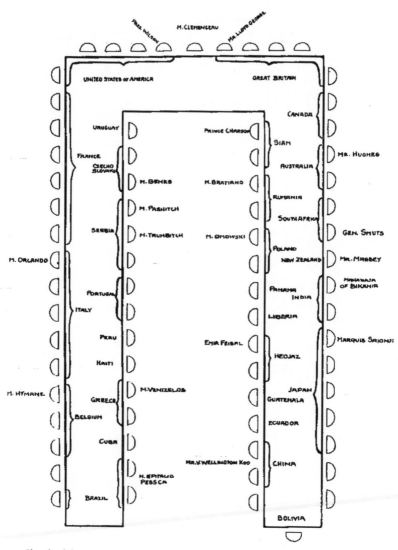

Sketch of the seating plan at the Paris Peace Conference.

5

Délégation du Royaume des Serbes, Croates et Slovènes

'Delegation of the Kingdom of Serbs, Croats and Slovenes'. That was the name on which members of the Yugoslav delegation at the Paris Peace Conference insisted in all communications. The Allies, on the other hand, referred to it officially as the delegation of the 'Kingdom of Serbia', despite the fact that the latter country no longer existed following the proclamation of the Kingdom of Serbs, Croats and Slovenes on 1 December 1918. Although the United States recognised the Yugoslav state in early February 1919 – after the Peace Conference had begun – Italy blocked the recognition by the Conference of the Serb-Croat-Slovene Kingdom. So, 'Yugoslavia', its exact territory as yet unknown, was to be 'Serbia', whether its representatives liked it or not. In contrast, two other post-Habsburg states, Czechoslovakia and Poland, were recognised at the very first session of the Peace Conference, held on 18 January.

Before Paris

The newly-formed South Slav state was in a precarious position in late 1918 and early 1919, and securing international recognition of its borders was vital for its survival. It was therefore crucially important to send a well-prepared and representative delegation, with an agreed set of goals and demands. Yet there was no time for serious preparations, and other, even more pressing, issues had to be dealt with by the provisional authorities. Within weeks of founding the country, an interim government and parliament were in place and the (Serbian) army tried to defend the borders and deal with rebellions and social discontent at home, mostly among ethnic Albanians, Montenegrins and Croats. A peace delegation was put together in haste and amid much uncertainty.

The pace of events necessitated this. The provisional government of the Kingdom of Serbs, Croats and Slovenes was formed on 20 December, and it selected key members of the peace delegation two days later. It was not for another week that all delegates were informed. Experts and other members of the wider delegation took even longer to select, inform and send to Paris. Delegates were still arriving there weeks after the Conference had convened.

Pašić had been seen as a logical choice for the post of Prime Minister by political leaders from all parts of the new country. He was chosen unanimously and without debate at a preliminary meeting of the leading politicians held in mid-December in the Belgrade home of Stojan Protić, Pašić's right-hand man. Neither Pašić nor Trumbić were in Belgrade to attend the meeting. Smodlaka and other leaders from the former Habsburg territories recommended Trumbić as Foreign Minister, but Protić immediately rejected the idea, convinced that Pašić would object. The Radicals objected to Trumbić, not to

Croats in general; Protić asked Smodlaka, a Dalmatian Croat politician who had played a major part in the unification of Yugoslavia, to accept the foreign affairs portfolio. Smodlaka refused, on the grounds of ill health.

Discussions over the composition of the provisional government continued over the next few days. Pašić did indeed object to Trumbić's nomination to the post of Foreign Minister, but eventually agreed, persuaded by Smodlaka and two other leaders of the Habsburg South Slavs: Svetozar Pribićević, a Serb, and Anton Korošec, a Slovene. Korošec was chosen as Deputy Prime Minister, while the Interior Ministry went to Pribićević. The key portfolios were intentionally distributed to leading representatives of various regions and 'tribes'. However, Prince Regent Alexander vetoed Pašić's nomination, instead giving the mandate to form a government to Protić. As if the Prince Regent wanted Pašić out of the country during the formative months of the new state, the Radical leader was chosen to lead the peace delegation in Paris, with Trumbić as his deputy. Pašić was not happy, but had little choice. Trumbić reluctantly agreed to serve as Foreign Minister for the duration of the Peace Conference only. (He would indeed resign soon after the Conference ended.)[1]

The delegation thus arrived in Paris without preparation and without a previously agreed strategy. Its members, however, were experienced politicians who, as time would show, coped admirably well under the circumstances. It certainly helped that Pašić's wartime government had begun collecting material for the post-war settlement before the end of the war. Pašić took this material with him when he left for Paris, which even included documents and papers the Serbian government had used at the 1878 Congress of Berlin.

Trumbić was similarly experienced and well-prepared, since the Yugoslav Committee had produced a number of publications, maps, documents and other propaganda material supporting the Yugoslav cause during the war. Yet, the lack of proper, joint preparation and especially the fact that the delegation went to Paris without previously-agreed compromise solutions would seriously hurt the team spirit among the delegates. When it came to maximalist territorial demands, the Yugoslavs were in agreement. However, ideal situations rarely present themselves at large international peace conferences. The Yugoslavs had to negotiate borders with as many as seven neighbours, and in all but one case (Greece), there were serious differences of opinion.

Recognition

The question of the recognition of an independent Yugoslav state was a complex one and had been raised even before Yugoslavia had been formed. In the summer of 1918, Pašić and Trumbić had disagreed over the latter's ultimately unsuccessful attempt to persuade the Allies to recognise the Yugoslav Committee as a government of the Habsburg South Slavs. The issue became even more pressing following the Italian occupation of Istria, Fiume and parts of Dalmatia at the end of the war. The Allies refused to recognise the State of Slovenes, Croats and Serbs, proclaimed in Zagreb at the end of October 1918, citing two reasons: first, the conditions of the Armistice must be carried out, and second, a common 'Serbian-Yugoslav' government should be formed. Matters were further complicated with the Act of Union on 1 December. Did Regent Alexander proclaim a new state or did he announce the extension of Serbia, which had not ceased to be a sovereign state?

Following the proclamation of Yugoslavia in Belgrade, and the formation of its first government a few weeks later, the country seemed to have fulfilled the main Allied criteria necessary to be considered a sovereign state. However, Italy's military presence on the ground and its diplomatic pressure on the Allies meant that the Yugoslav character of the Belgrade delegation was not recognised when the Peace Conference opened on 18 January 1919.

The Allies simultaneously ignored and tolerated the Yugoslav delegation in Paris. The Yugoslavs adopted a similarly ambiguous stand: they behaved as if their country was recognised, but accepted that for the time being they were regarded, officially at least, as representatives of pre-war Serbia. This was not necessarily a disadvantage, for the popularity and reputation of Serbia in 1919, especially in France, was considerable. Thanks to this, the Serb-Croat-Slovene delegation enjoyed a prestige higher than that of many other well-established countries, let alone a new state with a complex name that also included a former Austrian minister.

> 'It is a national calamity for a new state to be burdened with such an elephantine designation. Perhaps some national poet can invent a single nation word to meet the case.'
>
> SIR EYRE CROWE, ON THE NAME 'KINGDOM OF SERBS, CROATS AND SLOVENES', MAY 1919[2]

It may be argued that by tolerating the Yugoslav delegation, the Conference recognised the new state *de facto*, even before it did so *de jure* in May–June 1919. It cannot be argued, however – even though it is occasionally done to this day – that Yugoslavia was the creation of the Paris Peace Conference. The main obstacle to the independence of small East-Central European countries – Austria-Hungary – had disintegrated

TERMINOLOGY

Supreme War Council
Early Conference sessions were referred to as 'preliminary meetings of the Supreme War Council'. This terminology, coined by David Lloyd George, remained in use until March, when the 'Supreme War Council' gradually became the 'Peace Conference'.

Conference or Congress?
Essentially, there is no difference between the two terms, though a congress tends to have a more formal character. Therefore, Paris was more a congress than a conference, but the term 'conference' is the one usually associated with the event.

Council of Ten (January–March 1919)
Prime Ministers of Britain, France, Italy and the President of the USA with their respective Foreign Ministers, and two Japanese representatives.

Council of Four ('Big Four', March–June 1919) The Prime Ministers of Britain, France, Italy and the President of the USA. Sometimes, 'Big Three' was used to refer to the leaders of Britain, France and the USA.

Council of Five (after March 1919)
Foreign Ministers of Britain, France, Italy, Japan and the USA.

two months before the Conference convened. The Allies had indirectly helped the creation of Yugoslavia and other new and restored states by defeating the Habsburg Monarchy, but the Empire was destroyed from within as well as from without, and the national movements that emerged in the old Monarchy led to the creation of the successor states. In the case of Yugoslavia, Serbia played a major, if not decisive, role in the formation of the Serb-Croat-Slovene Kingdom. The Yugoslavs, like the Czechoslovaks and the Poles, presented the Conference with a fait accompli, but, unlike in the case of the latter two, the Yugoslav fait accompli was ignored.

While not opposing the creation of Yugoslavia, the Allies refused to recognise it. In fact, they even failed to formally recognise Serbia's unification with Montenegro, which took place on 26 November 1918, almost a week before a united Serb-Croat-Slovene Kingdom was proclaimed. The Conference reserved a seat for a representative of Montenegro – still independent in the eyes of its exiled King Nicholas and his supporters at home and abroad. In the event, the Montenegrin chair remained empty throughout the Conference.

Composition and structure

The Yugoslav delegation was clearly not exclusively Serbian, but Serbs predominated. The delegation's supreme body, the Political Section, was made up of seven members: three Serbs, two Croats and two Slovenes. Serb domination was more pronounced in the various sections of experts that made up the Yugoslav contingent; as a rule, these sections were headed by Serbs. This was partly because even before the unification of Yugoslavia Pašić's government had started choosing future delegates. Serbia, formerly an independent state, possessed a large number of experienced politicians, diplomats and civil servants. In retrospect, however, the predominance in Paris of Serbs from pre-1912 Serbia seems to have foreshadowed their domination of Yugoslavia throughout the inter-war period.

Pašić and other Serbian members of the delegation unquestionably saw themselves as representatives of the Serb-Croat-Slovene Kingdom; yet at the same time they felt themselves Serbia's representatives, regardless of the Allies' attitude. Already in January 1919 General Petar Pešić, an ethnic Serb and head of the Military Section, complained that a document drafted by Trumbić gave the impression that 'Serbia does not exist anymore', because Trumbić referred to 'former Serbia'. 'Austria-Hungary may be former, but Serbia is not', insisted the General.[3] This was the main reason why Pašić and most other – but not all – Serb leaders preferred the Kingdom of Serbs, Croats and Slovenes, rather than simply Kingdom of Yugoslavia, as the name for the state; Trumbić and many non-Serbs were in favour of 'Yugoslavia'. The argument over the name of the country went on during the Conference. For instance, Mateja Bošković, a member of the Political Section, the former minister to London and a member of Pašić's Radical Party, complained that Milenko Vesnić, a plenipotentiary (and a fellow Serb and Radical), had used the term 'Yugoslavia' in his presentation to the Council of Ten on 18 February.[4]

Milenko Vesnić (1862–1921), was the Prime Minister of the Kingdom of Serbs, Croats and Slovenes in 1920–1, and one of the country's delegates at the Paris Peace Conference, 1919–20. As a member of Pašić's Radical Party, Vesnić was elected to the Serbian parliament in 1893, the same year he was appointed a Professor of International Law at Belgrade University. In 1901 he served as Serbia's Minister to Rome, and was Belgrade's Minister to Paris between 1904 and 1920, the position to which he returned in 1921, shortly before his death.

Such an attitude may be understandable. General Pešić had spent his whole career serving in the Serbian army and fighting several wars, while Bošković had built his diplomatic career representing Serbia during the country's emergence as a regional power. Pašić was a major participant in the political events that had shaped Serbia from its independence from the Ottoman Empire in 1878, through the Balkan Wars and, ultimately, to victory in the First World War. He was, in the words of a contemporary, the very 'essence of Serbia'.[5] Such an attitude, however, was damaging to the unity of the new state. Pašić – like many other Serbs – did not seem to understand that Yugoslavia was a radically different state from old Serbia.[6]

The Serbs were not the only members of the delegation who were often guided by their sectarian instincts. Trumbić and Smodlaka were mostly interested in the fate of their native Dalmatia and of Fiume and Istria, while the Slovenes seemed to be largely concerned with acquiring as much 'Slovene land' in the north-west as possible, even when no Slovene presence could be objectively determined. When it became clear that the Yugoslavs could not get all the territories they wanted, the political delegates usually appeared more willing to sacrifice territory to which they were not personally attached. This, inevitably, led to disagreements within the delegation.

The internal disunity within the delegation did little to strengthen its negotiating position or the international standing of the new country. However, such disunity should not be overstated. Regardless of their sectarianism, members of the delegation were unquestionably also Yugoslav patriots; the two feelings were not necessarily mutually exclusive. The Yugoslavs in Paris were united in the belief that they were on a historic mission to secure internationally-recognised borders of a large and free South Slav state for the first time in their history. This is probably the reason why, despite all the internal bickering, they maintained a remarkable show of unity when communicating with other delegations.[7]

Belgrade sent a 110-member mission to Paris. It was the fourth largest delegation attending a Conference that was characterised by a large number (26 in total) of large delegations. Only the British, the French and the Italians outnumbered the Yugoslavs, who outnumbered the US delegation by two members. A conservative estimate puts the total number of delegates present in Paris in the spring of 1919 at just over 1,000, not counting plenipotentiaries and 'experts'. There were 70 plenipotentiaries and 34 'substitutes', as well as countless experts. The British delegation had some 200 members, who were staying in five hotels.[8]

If interpreters, translators, typists and other aides were included, the Yugoslav camp probably numbered around 300 people. The headquarters of the delegation were in the Hotel Beau-Site, Rue de Presbourg, near the Place de Étoile, where the political delegation met almost daily and where many delegates lived. Some delegates, including Pašić, were accompanied by their families.[9]

The structure of the Serb-Croat-Slovene delegation resembled that of other delegations in Paris.[10] At the top of the large pyramid was the Political Section (also referred to as the Political Delegation), consisting of seven delegates. Pašić, Trumbić, Vesnić and Ivan Žolger, who had been minister without portfolio in the Austrian government of 1918, were the plenipotentiaries, accredited to represent the delegation at the Conference sessions. The remaining three members – Bošković, Smodlaka and Otokar Ribarž, a leading Slovene politician – were officially the délégués du gouvernement; they took part in the decision-making of the Political Section, but were given no mandate to attend the Conference. The importance given to the plenipotentiaries was evident in their salaries: they received 250 French francs per day, while the government delegates' daily allowance was 150 francs. Heads of various sections received the same amount, while other members of the delegation were paid 100 francs per day.[11]

The vast majority of the delegation was made up of experts, diplomats and secretaries, responsible for military, naval, economic-financial, international legal and 'ethnographic-historic' affairs; there was also a press department and a section for Montenegrin affairs. The Montenegrin section was headed by Andrija Radović, who had played a crucial role in Montenegro's unification with Serbia in late

November 1918 and in the deposition of King Nicholas and his government. He was one of several non-members of the political delegation who periodically attended its meetings.

Most of the experts were academics, and most were Serbian. Arguably, the most influential among them was Professor Jovan Cvijić, an internationally-renowned authority on Balkan ethnography. Cvijić's influence is evident from various memoranda concerning territorial claims, especially in the north and east, which he either authored or co-authored. The Yugoslav *Memorandum on Claims*, presented on 18 February, 'bore obvious traces of the hand of M. Cvijić, the most learned and enlightened not only of Serbian, but of all Balkan geographic experts', wrote a British contemporary.[12] Professor Slobodan Jovanović, a leading Serbian historian and jurist, played a less obvious but highly influential role in the delegation, especially in issues concerning international law, war guilt and the League of Nations.[13]

Josip Smodlaka (1869–1956), was a Dalmatian Croat politician. As a member of the Party of Rights he was elected to the Dalmatian Assembly in 1901. One of the initiators of the 'New Course' which resulted in the Croat-Serb Coalition and a member of the National Council in Zagreb, he played a major part in the unification of Yugoslavia. A key member of the country's delegation in Paris, he resigned in 1920 over its failure to settle the Adriatic question. He was appointed Yugoslavia's Minister to the Vatican in 1923, a post from which he resigned in 1929. In 1943 he joined Tito's Partisan movement and participated in negotiations between Yugoslavia and Italy over the post-Second World War borders.

Members of the delegation, including the Political Section, changed throughout the Conference, so its size and membership varied. From December 1919 the number of Yugoslav peacemakers in Paris significantly decreased. Even the Political Section did not survive in its original, full membership – Bošković and Smodlaka eventually resigned due to their disagreements with the decisions taken by the delegation in relation to the Treaty of St Germain and negotiations with Italy respectively. In this respect, the Yugoslav delegation was not unusual: other delegations, too, experienced change of personnel, internal disagreements and resignations.

The Yugoslav delegation was unusual in another sense. The Conference was seen by contemporaries as a historic event that would shape the future of the world, by solving territorial disputes and thus preventing future ethnically-motivated conflicts. Even delegations of the Great Powers were led by Presidents or Prime Ministers: President Woodrow Wilson of the United States and Prime Ministers Georges Clemenceau of France, David Lloyd George of Great Britain and Vittorio Orlando of Italy led their countries' delegations (and were known in Paris as the 'Big Four'). Pašić, on the other hand, was a former Prime Minister of Serbia, with no portfolio in the first Yugoslav government. Trumbić may have been the Foreign Minister, but as such he could not make any important decisions without the consent of the government at home. Furthermore, all decisions were to be made on the principle of consensus; any member of the Political Section could veto any decision, in which case the government in Belgrade would act as an arbiter. With the government itself often lacking a unified view on matters discussed in Paris, some decisions took days to be made.

This would have slowed down the delegation's work under the best of circumstances. But, at a time when continental Europe was just emerging from the war, communications were especially slow. Telegrams between Paris and Belgrade had to go via Greece and Malta (the telegraph system through former Austria-Hungary had not yet been restored) and took at best two days to arrive. Couriers were used for the longer and most important documents, but they took even more time – four or five days – to reach their destination.

'Pašić and Trumbić! Seldom have circumstances bound two more antithetical characters to a common cause', wrote a historian of the Yugoslavia delegation in Paris. 'Seldom, indeed, have two antagonists been forced to become partners so quickly.'[14] Nevertheless, the choice of Pašić and Trumbić as the leaders of the delegation made sense. Pašić may have been without a government post in the newly-created Yugoslav state, but in 1919 he enjoyed great international prestige. He was a symbol of Serbian valour and of its significant contribution to the war effort. In those rare moments when he left the headquarters of the Yugoslav delegation, ordinary Parisians recognised him and greeted him in the streets, showing their appreciation of his and Serbia's contribution to victory. Pašić was also an extremely experienced and shrewd politician, and he appeared something of an enigma to foreign statesmen. 'Though never as popular in Western circles as Venizelos, Beneš, or Paderewski, he still enjoyed great prestige.'[15]

Pašić did not crave publicity, and instead preferred to work behind closed doors. Despite studying in Zurich and travelling around the Allied countries during the war, he did not seem to know much about the 'West', nor seem much interested in it. He was a man withdrawn into himself, whether he was dealing with his fellow Serbs or with foreigners. A contemporary later recalled how Pašić preferred to spend his free time at Corfu studying plants and enjoying nature.[16] Very few people were allowed into his private world. He preferred to spend evenings in Paris in his hotel room, in the company of his family, who accompanied him. Of all the leading statesmen in Paris, Pašić only met Clemenceau and Wilson once each (this, admittedly, also had much to do with the fact that the 'Big Four' rarely had time in Paris to receive leaders of the small nations, preferring to make major decisions without them). When not in a meeting, Pašić read newspapers – 'Belgrade dailies and a Parisian tabloid' – or talked privately with Vesnić, who often acted as his liaison with the Quai d'Orsay.[17]

The disadvantage of such an insular, if workaholic, routine in Paris was that Pašić possibly failed fully to exploit the Serbs', and his own, popularity at the time. But, it should be remembered that in 1919 he was already 74, with an eventful life behind him. It seemed as if Paris was to be the zenith of a remarkable political career, especially because of his conflict with Prince Regent Alexander.

'A gloomy man.'
HAROLD NICOLSON ON TRUMBIĆ[18]

Though to a lesser degree than Pašić, Trumbić, too, enjoyed a considerable international reputation. Before the war, he had distinguished himself in his role in the Yugoslav movement and his opposition to the former Dual Monarchy. As the leader of the exiled wartime Yugoslav Committee, he made international connections, especially among the British. Trumbić's inclusion in the government and in the delegation was also proof to the outside world that Croats were enthusiastic about the new state – despite Stjepan Radić's Peasant Party gathering support among the Croat masses for what appeared to be a separatist programme.

Like Pašić, Trumbić was a workaholic whose only real passion was politics. He, too, was a political conservative and a stubborn, strong-willed man. However, while Pašić often disguised his stubbornness by appearing to agree with his opponents, Trumbić usually preferred to speak out, even when no one else supported him. According to Smodlaka, Trumbić, even more than Pašić, felt the need to be seen as a leader. A discreet, yet obvious, dislike of Trumbić among the Serbian delegates undoubtedly made his position even more difficult. Trumbić's secretary – a Serb from Serbia – noted in his diary during the first weeks of the Conference that 'animosity towards Trumbić is increasingly felt'. Trumbić complained to his secretary that Vesnić kept him in the dark even on matters concerning the Adriatic, and that he was overwhelmed with documents written in Cyrillic, which he could read, but not as quickly as those written in the Latin alphabet.[19]

Although both Pašić and Trumbić were of humble origins, the latter was more accustomed to behaving like a 'European gentleman'. Trumbić was sociable and an excellent communicator, showing off his fluency in French and Italian. A Serbian student in Paris, who attended Trumbić's public lecture at the Sorbonne during the war, was deeply impressed with his excellent French and his 'Latin culture'. Younger and a better communicator than Pašić, Trumbić was an energetic man who regularly mingled with diplomats and journalists in Paris. His charisma and the power of his argument greatly helped the Yugoslav cause, especially with regard to the Adriatic question.[20] Yet, he was also temperamental and did not always impress others, as the quote by Harold Nicolson suggests.

As for the other members of the Political Section, Vesnić was also a logical choice. He was a seasoned diplomat with excellent contacts among the French and the Americans – his wife, an American heiress, was friendly with Mrs Wilson. Vesnić was widely considered to be the best speaker among the Yugoslavs, and had a reputation as a scholar as well as a diplomat. The selection of Ivan Žolger, on the other hand, seemed less logical. He was Deputy Prime Minister Anton Korošec's unofficial representative in Paris, but his past made him a questionable choice at the very least. As a former Austrian minister, Žolger's appointment to the Serb-Croat-Slovene delegation raised more than just eyebrows; the Italians in particular objected to his participation at the Conference.

None of the three délégues du gouvernement was in fact a member of the government. Bošković was a former minister to London, whose loyalty to Pašić was apparently only matched by his taste for Savile Row suits. Smodlaka and Ribarž were the leading pro-Yugoslav Croat and Slovene politicians, respectively. Both were former deputies in the Vienna parliament, where they had advocated the Yugoslav cause, and both were prominent and popular public figures. Smodlaka had also played a major role in the events of late November 1918 which led to the unification of Yugoslavia. All in all, the Yugoslavs had sent a competent and 'very strong' panel to Paris.[21]

Ivan Žolger (1867–1925), was a minister without portfolio in the last Austrian government in 1918. Prior to that, he was a civil servant in the Austrian Ministry of Education and in the government in 1917–18. A plenipotentiary delegate in the delegation of the Kingdom of Serbs, Croats and Slovenes at the Paris Peace Conference, afterwards he became a Law Professor at the University of Ljubljana.

Allies and Rivals

The first meeting of the delegation took place on 10 January 1919, at the Hotel Campbell, where Pašić had been staying since his arrival in the French capital a few days previously. The Yugoslavs did not appear before the Supreme Council until 31 January, when at very short notice they were asked to state their claims to the Banat region (formerly part of Hungary, now in north-east Serbia and north-west Romania). They did not get an opportunity to present their full territorial claims until 18 February, exactly a month after the Conference had begun. However, the Yugoslav delegates and experts were busy meeting on an almost daily basis, discussing, debating and preparing memoranda on territorial claims, drawing maps and living in an atmosphere of great expectations and even greater uncertainties. The question on everyone's minds during the first months of the Conference was: when would the Serb-Croat-Slovene state gain recognition, and with what borders would it emerge from the Paris settlement?

No one within the Serb-Croat-Slovene delegation knew when the country's borders would be discussed. On 18 January, the delegation met twice, before and after the opening session of the Conference, attended by Pašić, Trumbić and Vesnić. At both meetings, the question of frontiers with Italy arose, and divisions within the delegation that would plague its work throughout the Conference clearly emerged.

During the morning meeting Trumbić suggested that the withdrawal of Italian troops from the eastern Adriatic must be demanded, because the occupation had lost its *raison d'être* with the demise of Austria-Hungary; the Serb-Croat-Slovene state was capable of controlling the territory currently held by the Italians. Vesnić immediately objected, believing that such a demand had no chance of success and would merely irritate the Allies. Smodlaka sided with Trumbić, and Bošković with Vesnić. Pašić kept quiet, but it is not hard to guess where his sympathies rested: throughout the Conference, he sought to avoid confrontation with the Allies.

It was the second meeting of the delegation that day, which started at 9.00 p.m., that exposed fundamental differences between Pašić and Trumbić concerning territorial claims. Pašić believed the delegation should base its claims on geo-strategic grounds as well as on the nationality principle, while

Trumbić thought national self-determination should be the main, if not the sole principle on which to base territorial claims. Smodlaka, who did not enjoy a close personal relationship with Trumbić but who had not hidden his admiration for Pašić, spoke out in support of Trumbić. By employing other than ethnic arguments, 'we will facilitate and lend justification to Italian claims in Dalmatia', he warned, 'and will, moreover, incur retribution in the future'.[22]

Pašić listened carefully and then responded, speaking slowly and quietly, as usual. The reply captures his thinking extremely well. *It is important to adhere to the principle of nationality*, Pašić said, *but even from this point of view our claims are justified and to the ultimate limit of possibility this principle will be maintained. Italian claims against us, as an Allied country, cannot be equalled with our demands against enemies. Our demands for a rectification of the frontier with Bulgaria do not violate that principle, as is also the case with our claims in the Banat, where we are in conflict with the Rumanians who have no right to the Banat, if one holds strictly to the principle of nationality.* In Pašić's view, it was impossible to create borders based entirely on ethnicity: *A political frontier cannot be drawn strictly along an ethnographic line, because the nationalities are mixed, and as much as we might receive of a foreign element so much of ours will have to go to the others.*[24]

General Pešić supported Pašić, arguing, correctly as it turned out, that all delegations would try to get as much territory as possible and that the Yugoslavs should not therefore demand anything less than their maximum aims. Bošković and Ribarž agreed.

'One of the craftiest and most tenacious statesmen in South Eastern Europe.'
LLOYD GEORGE ON PAŠIĆ[23]

The following day the debate continued. Since no agreement on a final draft could be reached, and since the Council of Ten might summon the delegation any day, Pašić recommended that the delegation adopt General Pešić's document, based on maximalist aims, as a provisional draft. He once again spoke in support of 'Serb' and 'Slovene' claims. As for borders with Italy, *where we must come to agreement, I wish to hear your views*, Pašić told the delegates. Trumbić and Smodlaka must have felt Pašić was trying to outmanoeuvre them by creating a Serb-Slovene axis within the delegation.[25]

Whether Pašić intended to forge such an alliance within the delegation or not, he was mainly concerned with the borders with Bulgaria, Romania and Hungary. He was perfectly happy for the Slovenes to take the lead in respect of borders with Austria and most probably would have been equally content to let Trumbić and Smodlaka take charge of the border with Italy. However, Italy's competing claims threatened the Yugoslav overall demands, and Pašić feared that extensive Yugoslav claims in the Adriatic might antagonise Britain and France. Marshal Foch had told him personally the day before the Conference officially opened that the Yugoslavs should not ask for Trieste (Trst) and Pola (Pula), and that Fiume should be a free state. Pašić allegedly rejected the latter suggestion, but clearly feared that extensive demands in the Adriatic could weaken his bargaining position in the north-east and east.[26]

Trumbić, on the other hand, was concerned that quite the opposite would happen: that demands in Bulgaria and the Banat would compromise the Yugoslavs' position in their negotiations with Italy. He suggested that ethnographic experts be consulted about borders, recommending a group of Serbian professors led by Cvijić. Did he hope to use Serbian experts in order to undermine Pašić's arguments?[27]

After further debate, Trumbić had his way. It was decided, oddly, that all the political delegates but the three highest-ranked ones – Pašić, Trumbić and Vesnić – would meet with the experts the following day and draw up an ethnographic map of the Yugoslav nation.[28]

So, as the Conference commenced, the Yugoslavs stood divided. Trumbić and Smodlaka favoured the nationality principle. Pašić and the Serb members of the political delegation clearly thought a combination of ethnic and strategic criteria should be used. The Slovenes appeared to be somewhere between the two positions, though probably closer to Pašić than to Trumbić. They shared the Croats' belief in adhering to the nationality principle because they wanted Trieste. Yet, their claims in Austria did not always meet the nationality criteria. Trumbić and Smodlaka were irritated by the excessive demands of the Slovenes, which threatened to undermine the Yugoslav argument against Italy over the eastern Adriatic. Scholars tend to concentrate on Serb-Croat differences when writing about Yugoslavia, but in Paris, differences between Croats and Slovenes were just as important. The Croats felt the Slovenes acted selfishly, but managed to get away with it by siding with the Serbs. Smodlaka later recalled how the Slovene delegates had separate offices and were *de facto* a delegation within the delegation. Žolger, alone among the plenipotentiaries, had his own, separate secretariat. Unlike the Croats and Serbs, the Slovenes were well-organised, united and worked tirelessly. According to Smodlaka, it looked from the outside as if Slovenia were an independent state within the Yugoslav protectorate.[29]

The question of borders and the likely opposition from Italy and Romania to Yugoslav claims preoccupied the delegates during the early stages of the Conference. At the same time, news about local tensions and conflicts in Istria, Dalmatia and the Banat were arriving from the country on an almost daily basis. The news undoubtedly put additional strain on the delegates. Because they did not know when the Conference would discuss their claims and were usually summoned by the Council at very short notice, they must have worked under enormous pressure and anxiety. The Allied attitude was caused partly by the chaos, partly by a general ignorance of the needs of small nations, which was characteristic in Paris, especially during the first few months of the Conference, and partly by a tendency of the Big Four to work behind closed doors. 'Nobody knows anything because everything is happening behind the scenes', observed a French diplomat.[30] In such an atmosphere, tensions between Pašić and Trumbić may be understandable. Their wartime animosity would have probably reappeared even under the best of circumstances, let alone in the conditions under which they worked.

However, it is important to keep in mind that Yugoslav differences did not always run across the 'ethnic' divide. Smodlaka and Trumbić, for instance, did not see eye to eye, while there were divisions among Serb members and also between Žolger and Ribarž; at times Trumbić and the government in Belgrade stood opposite Pašić, at other times Pašić and Trumbić disagreed with the government. Neither did the Yugoslavs have a monopoly over disunity. Almost every other delegation suffered from internal bickering and resignations, victorious and defeated alike: Italians, British, Romanians, Germans, Bulgarians... Perhaps most famously, Wilson and Colonel House fell out to such an extent that after Paris these once closest of friends never spoke to each other again. The clash of Wilsonian principles and the old diplomacy, which contributed to the conflict between Trumbić and Pašić, was also a main divisive issue among the Allies. It is too easy, especially in retrospect, to point out ethnic rivalries as undermining Yugoslavia from the very start. The Yugoslavs in Paris were allies *and* rivals, but alliances and rivalries existed within other delegations as well as across the Conference.

6
Claims and Expectations

A popular saying in the former Yugoslavia was that the country was surrounded by 'BRIGAMA' (literally, 'by worries' – an acronym of the initial letters of the names of Yugoslavia's neighbours: Bulgaria, Romania, Italy, Greece, Albania, Hungary [Madjarska in Serbo-Croat] and Austria). The saying reflected a small state's paranoia, but it also had grounds in reality, certainly in 1919, when all the neighbours apart from Greece disputed Yugoslavia's borders (and some would continue to do so long after the Peace Conference). It was probably to be expected that the defeated countries, like Bulgaria, or those with a large minority inside the South Slav kingdom, such as Albania and Hungary, would challenge Yugoslavia's territorial claims in 1919–20. The real challenge, however, came from its wartime allies, Romania and especially Italy. The status of Montenegro was both an internal and international affair, and was related to the Italo-Yugoslav conflict.

Italy

On 11 March 1919 Josip Smodlaka gave a lecture in Paris, presenting the official claims of the Yugoslav delegation. 'Besides the late Kingdoms of Serbia and Montenegro it [the Kingdom of Serbs, Croats and Slovenes] comprises the former Austro-Hungarian provinces of Croatia, Slavonia, Bosnia and Herzegovina, which constitute the nucleus of our national territory and hence cannot be under any circumstances denied [to] the State of Serbs, Croats and Slovenes', Smodlaka stated. The Yugoslavs made up over 90 percent of the population of these lands, and, crucially, the 'nucleus' of Yugoslavia did not 'touch upon the ethnic domain of neighbouring peoples'. He then listed 'fringe' territories that the Kingdom of Serbs, Croats and Slovenes claimed on the basis of national self-determination, starting with those in the eastern Adriatic:

1. The Province of Dalmatia (630,000 inhabitants, of whom 97 per cent are Jugoslavs, and 3 per cent Italians).
2. The Town of Reka [*sic*] (Fiume) with 50,000 inhabitants, Jugoslavs and Italians.
3. The Eastern part of the former Austrian littoral (Istria, Trieste and Gorica without the Gradisca region) with 780,000 inhabitants, of whom 55 per cent are Jugoslavs and 37 per cent Italians.[1]

Other territories which the delegation demanded included the Banat, the neighbouring Bačka, as well as the Austrian provinces of Styria and Carniola.

Members of the Serb-Croat-Slovene delegation insisted that the eastern Adriatic belonged to Yugoslavia by virtue of a South Slav majority.[2] Italian claims to Dalmatia, Fiume and

Istria, on the other hand, rested more on practical and sentimental reasons than on the principle of nationality.

The Italians argued that it was in their strategic interest to obtain Dalmatia, which historically and culturally had been part of the Italian world. The direct and indirect (through the Albanian protectorate) control of the eastern Adriatic coast would establish Italy's naval and economic primacy in the region. In 1915, the Italian Foreign Minister Sidney Sonnino believed that a hostile Austria-Hungary would continue to exist, even if it lost some territory. He also thought that an enlarged Serbia would emerge from the war, posing another challenge to Italy's domination in the region. Moreover, through a powerful Serbia, Russia's influence in the region would in all likelihood grow. Even if he could have envisaged the creation of a Yugoslavia back in 1915, his thinking would have been similar. Prime Minister Orlando complained during the Peace Conference that 'to our hurt and embarrassment, Yugoslavia will have taken the place of Austria, and everything will be as unsatisfactory as before'.[3]

Dalmatia was an ancient Roman province, which in more recent times had been under Venetian rule. The region, however, played little or no role in the development of Italian nationalism in the 19th century. Italian revolutionaries were more interested in Istria, and believed in the importance of Italian-Slav cooperation against Austria. As the 19th-century Italian nationalist leader Giuseppe Mazzini declared, 'Istria is Italian and as necessary to Italians as Dalmatia is to Slavs'.[4] On the other hand, it was in Dalmatia and Fiume that Croat-Serb political cooperation, with Trumbić and Smodlaka among the leaders, emerged in the early 20th century.

The 'Adriatic Question' – a territorial settlement with Italy – was arguably the most serious challenge that the delegation of the Kingdom of Serbs, Croats and Slovenes faced at the Conference. As one of the victorious powers, Italy was a member of the Council of Ten/Four which effectively ran the Conference. As explained previously, the Italians successfully lobbied other Powers regarding the question of the recognition of the Serb-Croat-Slovene state and its delegation. The strongest Italian card was probably the 1915 Treaty of London, which promised them territories in the eastern Adriatic in exchange for their entry into the war on the Allied side. If this dealt them a significant advantage, it also helped that their opponent faced the problem of internal disunity, in no small part caused by disagreements within the Yugoslav delegation over how to deal with the Adriatic question. All things considered, the Italians were the favourites to achieve their goals in the Adriatic. It would turn out that the Italo-Yugoslav dispute could not be solved in Paris, but only at specially convened talks in Rapallo, in north-west Italy, in late 1920.

The Question of Montenegro

The exiled King Nicholas of Montenegro, and Montenegrin leaders loyal to him, were Italy's natural allies. Rome would much rather have seen a small, independent Montenegro, which it could control by a combination of economic incentives, political pressures and close dynastic ties (Nicholas's daughter Helen married King Victor Emanuel III of Italy), than a large Yugoslav state which had absorbed tiny Montenegro. Since Montenegro had been incorporated into Yugoslavia, the Italians hoped it would destabilise the new state.

However, the Montenegrin question was more than merely part of a wider struggle between Italy and Yugoslavia over the eastern Adriatic. It was also among the most serious internal problems the young state faced. Supporters of the exiled

Montenegrin king, usually referred to as 'federalists' or the 'Greens', openly rebelled against the new authorities, and there were armed clashes with the 'unionists', also known as the 'Whites', and the gendarmerie in the months following unification.

The reasons for this internal division among Montenegrins lay largely in the modern history of the region. The idea of unification between Serbia and Montenegro went in parallel with the Yugoslav idea. In some ways, it was a more realistic short- to medium-term aim than the creation of Yugoslavia. Unlike a Yugoslavia, a Serb-Montenegrin union seemed a real possibility in the early 20th century.

Serbia and Montenegro had both been granted independence from the Ottoman Empire at the Congress of Berlin in 1878. As much as one can talk about national identities among Balkan peasants in the 19th century, the Eastern Orthodox populations of the two states felt overwhelmingly Serbian. Serbia and Montenegro shared a medieval history and many national myths, and, as a result of the 1912–13 Balkan Wars, a border; their populations spoke the same language. Post-1913 Montenegro included parts of Kosovo where in the Middle Ages the Serbian Orthodox Church had at one time had its principal seat. At that time King Nicholas dreamt of restoring the medieval Serbian Empire under his leadership.

Montenegro and Serbia united on 26 November 1918 – a week before the Kingdom of Serbs, Croats and Slovenes was proclaimed. Effectively, Serbia incorporated its smaller sister-kingdom, and the Petrović dynasty was overthrown. Divisions among Montenegrins between those who supported a union with Serbia and those who preferred the preservation of Montenegro under the Petrović dynasty, long predated 1918. These were not divisions imposed by a sense of 'ethnic' distinctiveness. The Croats may have invented the Yugoslav idea, and many of their leaders may have adhered to the ideology of 'national oneness', but at the same time there is no doubt that they also felt distinctly Croat. Montenegro, like Croatia, possessed a state tradition. 'Unlike the Croats, however, the Montenegrins also had a strong tradition of not just belonging to, but indeed leading the Serb people, something that mitigated their feeling of separateness', as a leading historian of Yugoslavia has argued.[5]

Following Montenegro's surrender in 1916 and a failed attempt to negotiate a dynastic union with Serbia, Andrija Radović formed the Montenegrin Committee for National Unification in Geneva in February 1917. From then on, Pašić dealt with the Committee only, boycotting the exiled Montenegrin government based in France (first in Bordeaux, then Neuilly). Nicholas's position further weakened with the overthrow of the Russian monarchy in February 1917; another one of his daughters had been married to a Romanov grand duke. In August 1917, Radović's Committee publicly supported the Pašić-Trumbić Declaration of Corfu, stating that 'with this war Montenegro is ending its role as a separate Serb state'. In October 1918, Nicholas called for a 'Yugoslav confederation', but the Serb leadership rejected the call, as did the Croat and Slovene politicians, who regarded the question of Montenegro as an 'internal' Serb affair.[6]

However, the status of Montenegro became an international problem in Paris. Nicholas and his supporters may have been largely abandoned by the French and the British, but to Italy they presented an additional argument against the Yugoslav claims. While the Podgorica Assembly in Montenegro had been working towards the union with Serbia during November 1918, Nicholas and his entourage had campaigned hard to maintain – or restore – an independent Montenegro. The Montenegrin King, supported by Italy, appointed Jovan Plamenac to be the Prime Minister of the Montenegrin government-in-exile. Plamenac officially asked the Peace Conference to allow Montenegro to take part. Nicholas and his exiled government published documents containing their territorial demands, asking for territory in Dalmatia, around Dubrovnik, and Herzegovina, 'envisaged' for Montenegro by the Treaty of London.[7] Not only Nicholas and Plamenac, but, just as significantly, the Italian government also refused to recognise the decisions of the Podgorica Assembly. The Italians argued, not without foundation, that the Assembly had acted under Serbia's instructions and that the decisions did not reflect the popular will. In Italy's view, the union was illegal, since it was carried out without the approval of the King and his government.

At the time when the Yugoslav delegates in Paris learned that they would not be recognised as representatives of the Kingdom of Serbs, Croats and Slovenes, and that they would be allowed only two seats at the Conference (later increased to three), they were also told that Montenegro would be allocated one seat. It fell to Pašić to inform his colleagues of these decisions on 14 January, which clearly dealt a serious blow to the Yugoslavs.[8] The refusal to recognise the Serb-Croat-Slovene delegation combined with the decision to grant a seat to Montenegro meant that in early 1919 the Allies essentially challenged the very existence of the Yugoslav union.

Had it not been for the Italian initiative, it is unlikely the Allies would have considered the exiled Montenegrin government's request for representation at the Conference. As early as 1916, an official of the British Foreign Office allegedly stated that an independent Montenegro in the post-war order would 'serve no useful purpose'. Although President Wilson did indeed talk about the restoration of Montenegro in his Fourteen Points – a fact cited by Nicholas and his Italian allies – neither the Americans, nor the British and the French, thought the question of Serb-Montenegrin union to be one of any real significance. What mattered to them was that Montenegro was no longer occupied by the Central Powers; whether it was to be restored as an independent state or incorporated into Serbia or Yugoslavia mattered considerably less.[9]

Romania

On 31 January 1919 the Yugoslavs were suddenly summoned by the Council of Ten to present their case for the Banat. Pašić, Trumbić and Vesnić attended. Despite their internal disagreements, the Yugoslavs presented a united front.

They questioned the validity of the secret Treaty of Bucharest, signed in August 1916, on the same grounds they disputed the secret Treaty of London: Serbia was not privy to the Treaty, nor it had been informed of its contents. 'As far as we are concerned [the Bucharest Treaty] does not exist since we do not even know about it', Vesnić told the Council. When Clemenceau objected that surely, the Treaty had not been kept a secret from Serbia, Pichon admitted that it had.[10]

The Banat had a mixed population comprising mostly Romanians, Serbs, Hungarians and Germans. The Yugoslavs claimed western and central parts of the region, using a combination of ethnic, historical, economic and strategic arguments.[11] The Romanians demanded the whole region. Their Prime Minister Ionel Brătianu argued that, with 600,000 Romanians, as opposed to 400,000 Germans and 300,000 Serbs, the Banat was ethnically predominantly Romanian; a partition of the region would be 'unnatural' because of its economic-geographic unity; and last, but not least, he pointed out that the Treaty of Bucharest promised the region to Romania. The complexity of the region, and the resulting lengthy presentations by the rival delegates – Brătianu complained afterwards that some members of the Council of Ten fell asleep while he was presenting – did not amuse some Council members. Yet the Romanians had powerful allies in Orlando and Sonnino, who, for obvious reasons, supported the validity of the 1916 Treaty of Bucharest. In fact, the Italians and the Romanians had made a secret deal to support each other against challenges to the two wartime secret treaties, as a British journalist had found out through a Romanian contact.[12] Once again, wartime secret diplomacy, which helped win the war, proved an obstacle in a peace that was supposed to be built on just, ethnic borders. The Allies were again facing the consequences of their secret diplomacy and had, once again, to compromise between pragmatism and idealism.

Different ethnicities, religions and languages were mixed to such an extent that no matter where borders were drawn the principle of national self-determination would have to be violated. The area claimed by the Yugoslavs had some 327,500 Slavs, of whom nearly 250,000 were Serbs (the rest were Czechs, Slovaks, Ruthenians and Slovenes). By comparison, there were between 213,000 and 246,000 Romanians in the same area (depending on the source).[13] The Yugoslavs argued that there had been strong historical and cultural links between the Banat and Serbia ever since a large number of Serbs had migrated to the region in the 17th century. In Trumbić's words, the Banat had *for centuries been the foyer of Serbian culture*, where nearly 300,000 Serbs lived.[14] Members of the Yugoslav delegation claimed that this former

Habsburg region had stronger economic ties with Serbia than with Romania. The region was strategically vital as its control would have strengthened the defence of Belgrade considerably. The capital city had been exposed to attacks from the north-west, a geo-strategic weakness the Central Powers had exploited during the war. The Yugoslavs also argued that, in any case, the Banat as a region had never had defined borders, so that it was not clear what area Romania actually claimed. Finally, they pointed out that since Romania had signed a separate peace with Austria-Hungary in Bucharest in May 1918, the 1916 Treaty of Bucharest with the Entente had automatically become invalid and should not be even discussed.

During the war Pašić had attempted to reach an agreement with the Romanians over the Banat. To that effect he had met with Take Ionescu, a Romanian minister, in Paris in October 1918. Ionescu had advocated the Romanian case in the Allied capitals, following the separate peace treaty between Romania and Austria-Hungary. With Prime Minister Eleftherios Venizelos of Greece acting as mediator, Pašić and Ionescu had agreed that the Banat should be partitioned between Romania and the future Yugoslav state, with Romania getting a larger portion.[15] However, Brătianu rejected the agreement, so two future founding members of the Little Entente – an alliance between Czechoslovakia, Romania and Yugoslavia formed in 1921 in order to check Hungarian revisionism – went to the Peace Conference as rivals.

The Banat question contributed to divisions within the Yugoslav delegation. During discussions on territorial claims within the Yugoslav delegation in late January 1919, Pašić argued, in regard to the Banat, that political borders did not necessarily coincide with ethnic borders because self-determination could not be always implemented in practice. He pointed out that Serbs, Hungarians and Romanians were intermixed to such an extent that no total separation was possible. Moreover, the Banat Germans were too detached territorially from Germany to ever conceivably be able to join their nation-state. Pašić argued that this meant that while many non-Yugoslavs would inevitably end up in Yugoslavia, some Yugoslavs would remain outside the borders of the Serb-Croat-Slovene Kingdom. The Serb and the Slovene delegates agreed with Pašić's arguments, but Smodlaka objected, repeating his – and Trumbić's – view that the delegation should only ask for territories unquestionably Yugoslav in terms of ethnicity and refuse to give those up even if pressured by the Allies.[16]

In the end, a compromise between Yugoslavia and Romania was reached during the summer of 1919, but not after much tension and the very real possibility of a military confrontation.

Hungary

Bačka and Baranja – like the Banat – were former Hungarian regions with an ethnic mix that meant drawing borders according to nationality was virtually impossible. Unlike in the case of the Banat, the Yugoslav claims in these two regions were disputed by defeated Hungary. This meant that the obstacle would be considerably smaller, though not straightforward.

The two regions were populated by three major groups: Hungarians (256,000), Germans (238,000) and Serbs (217,000). In addition, there were also between 150,000 and 180,000 *Bunjevci* and *Šokci*, Serbo-Croat speaking Catholic Slavs. Regardless of whether these two groups were actually Croats or Serbs or an entirely separate ethnicity – a debate that continues to this day – their presence ensured that the South Slavs were the largest group in the disputed territories. (The Slav presence was even stronger if nearly 70,000 Slovaks and some 14,000 Ruthenians were included.)[17] As in the case of the Banat, the Yugoslav delegation employed a combination of historic, economic and geo-strategic arguments to support its claims. Baranja and Bačka were described as centres of Serbian culture and religion, following the Serb migrations from the Ottoman Empire in previous centuries. Bačka's fertile land was also seen as vital for the young Yugoslav state, while both Baranja and Bačka were home to important rail and water routes the Yugoslavs were interested in. Finally, the Yugoslavs claimed two small, mostly Croat- and Slovene-populated pockets north of the Drava River (traditionally the border between Hungary and Croatia), known as Medjumurje and Prekomurje.

Bulgaria

The main conflict between Serbia and Bulgaria in the late 19th and early 20th centuries had been over Macedonia. Serbia (and Greece) had come out with the lion's share of the historic region at the expense of Bulgaria following the Second Balkan War of 1913. During the First World War, the Bulgarians temporarily regained the area, which they regarded as ethnically, culturally and historically Bulgarian, but at the end of the war Serbia/Yugoslavia recovered the lost territory.[18] So, with the Macedonian question seemingly settled in Belgrade's favour, the Yugoslav delegation demanded an extension into Bulgaria, along the old Serbian-Bulgarian border.

The Yugoslavs claimed this territory not so much on ethnic as on strategic grounds: as the war had shown, Serbian defences and the transport system in eastern parts of the country were vulnerable to Bulgarian attacks. An additional strip of territory would significantly strengthen Yugoslavia's defence against its potentially hostile eastern neighbour.

Pašić behaved towards Bulgaria as the leader of a victorious power which should be rewarded for its victory with additional territory of strategic importance, at the expense of its eastern neighbour and former enemy. As a native of eastern Serbia, Pašić's views were shaped by Serb-Bulgarian rivalry and the recent experiences of brutal Bulgarian occupation of parts of Serbia during the wars of 1912–18.

Pašić allegedly believed that for a stable and peaceful Balkans, as well as for the fulfillment of Serbian national goals, a Serb-Greek alliance should be established, and that it should prevail over a Bulgaro-Albanian axis. Having unsuccessfully explored the possibility of a Serb-Bulgarian rapprochement in the 1880s and in 1905–6, he was convinced, especially after the Balkan Wars and Sofia's attack on Belgrade in 1915, that Bulgaria must be isolated in the Balkans by Serbia/Yugoslavia and Greece.[19] In Paris, Pašić was determined that Bulgaria should be punished and weakened to the extent that it would never again be in a position to invade Serbia.

Despite the official rhetoric about the supposed 'South Serbian' identity of the Macedonian Slavs and claims of historical rights in Kosovo and Sandžak, Pašić was undoubtedly aware that the ethnic balance in these regions was not in the Serbs' favour. In other words, post-1912 Serbia had no longer been an ethnically homogenous nation-state. Did Pašić and the Serb delegates fear the re-opening of the Macedonian question at the Conference? Considering that Bulgaria was a defeated enemy, it was highly unlikely, but the prospect evidently crossed the Yugoslav delegates' minds. Trumbić, objecting to Pašić and Bošković's claims over Bulgaria – the latter even argued that western Bulgaria was ethnically Serbian – pointed out at the session held on 26 January that such tactics could prove counterproductive and could well open up the Macedonian question. Trumbić agreed with Pašić that it was important to secure Belgrade by obtaining an additional strip of land along the old Serbo-Bulgarian border, but he strongly objected to abusing the nationality principle for this purpose. He did not explain how the two goals could be reconciled, but proposed that the matter be referred to Belgrade if the delegates were unable to come to an agreement. Pašić, whom everyone expected to confront Trumbić, simply agreed with his Croat colleague as regarded the reason for claims in Bulgaria, but said nothing of the proposal to refer the matter to the government. Smodlaka and Ribarž also expressed their agreement that Belgrade, as the capital city, must be protected from a future land invasion. Vesnić then suggested that claims towards Bulgaria be adopted since there was a broad agreement now within the delegation, before declaring, perhaps hopefully, that the Macedonian question 'will never arise'.[20]

Vesnić's statement showed that there was a sense of anxiety within the delegation lest the Macedonian question be raised at the Conference. Smodlaka repeated the opinion previously expressed by Trumbić that excessive claims in Bulgaria could inadvertently strengthen Italy's demands in Istria and Dalmatia. The Italians could legitimately argue that if Yugoslavia claimed territories Yugoslavs did not inhabit, then Italy could employ arguments other than the nationality principle. Therefore, the delegation should request only territories that were indisputably South Slav. 'As we behave towards the Bulgarians, so the Italians will behave towards us', Smodlaka warned again. He rejected the claim – now also supported by General Pešić – that the population in the Bulgarian territories was ethnically Serb, arguing that circumstances had changed: the old Serbian ethnographic studies were no longer appropriate, while the current Foreign Minister (Trumbić) had different views on Bulgaria than his *de facto* predecessor (Pašić).[21]

In a typically shrewd move, Pašić appeared to agree with Smodlaka and suggested that Bulgaria's borders should be decided by the Conference. As for the position of the delegation, since no agreement could be found, Pašić suggested, and others agreed, to refer the matter to the government in Belgrade. If the Conference demanded the Yugoslavs' view before the government could send its response, the maximalist aims would be proposed.[22] Thus, after a long debate which failed to bring about a consensus, Pašić in fact indirectly imposed his view on Trumbić and Smodlaka. The Macedonian question would indeed be raised by the Allies indirectly, when they would insist that the Serb-Croat-Slovene delegation sign the treaty for the protection of minorities, largely with Macedonia in mind.

Albania

In essence, the main Yugoslav demand *vis-à-vis* Albania was that an independent Albanian state, established in 1913, should be preserved. Here, the rivalry with Italy offers an explanation for Belgrade's position. The relationship between Serbia and Italy had been further strained in June 1917 when the latter turned Albania into its protectorate. Despite French protests, the Italians had refused to back down, so Serbian troops had occupied parts of northern Albania, including the strategically important town of Scutari, which Montenegro desired. The Serbo-Montenegrin claims on the region rested on dubious historical and even less convincing ethnic claims. Although Scutari occupies a prominent place in the romantic-nationalist Serbo-Montenegrin interpretation of history, Belgrade wished above all to reduce Italian presence in the Balkans as much as possible. It was mainly for that reason that the Yugoslavs preferred to see an independent Albania rather than an Italian protectorate in its place. During the Conference, Albanian guerrillas, armed and encouraged by the Italians, regularly clashed with Yugoslav border troops and gendarmerie, who also had to deal with an armed insurrection among Yugoslav Albanians.

Although the preservation of an Albanian state was the Yugoslav official position, in reality, things were more complicated. Smodlaka, Žolger and Ribarž probably genuinely believed that the Albanians should receive Scutari on the nationality principle. Trumbić did too, and he feared that incorporating even more ethnic Albanians would destabilise the South Slav state. However, he was also of the opinion that Yugoslavia should receive Dalmatia and Istria *as well as* Scutari, as a 'compensation' for Serbia's sacrifices in the war and as a means of reducing Italian influence in the region. Compensation in northern Albania was also the recommendation of a group of American experts in January 1919, and Wilson did not object to the idea. Trumbić was therefore possibly being strategic – throughout the Conference he positioned himself close to the American President, the Yugoslavs' main ally in their contest with Italy. Pašić's thinking was even more complex. If the terms of the Treaty of London were to prevail in the end and Italy were to get its way, Rome would not only receive the Yugoslav-populated territory in the eastern Adriatic, but also large parts of Albania. In that case, the Serb-Croat-Slovene state would demand Scutari as a 'consolation prize' for losing Fiume.

In the early months of 1920, with the relationship between Wilson and the Yugoslav delegation increasingly distant, and not just because the President had left Paris, Pašić realised that Yugoslavia would not get Fiume, but believed that it could receive Scutari instead. The British and the French did not give him much reason to think otherwise. Even if the Treaty of London was not to be implemented, Pašić thought that Italy would eventually attempt to take over Albania, a development he thought would present Yugoslavia with an excellent opportunity to annex northern Albania. Pašić and Trumbić therefore differed in their prognosis for and tactics over Fiume, but both believed that Scutari should be accepted if offered. Only the Montenegrin Radović openly asked that the delegation should demand Scutari and northern Albania.[23] In the end, the Yugoslavs received neither Scutari nor Fiume, while the Albanian-Yugoslav border would be formally settled only in 1926.

Austria

Yugoslav demands in Lower Styria and Carinthia clashed with those of Austria. Although technically a new state, Austria was the core territory of a defeated former enemy. Seemingly, the ethnic mix here was less complex, and the Yugoslavs asked for the linguistic border between Slovene and German speakers to be turned into a political boundary. Yet, two problems emerged. First, the border was not so clear cut; for example, four predominantly German-speaking towns – Klagenfurt (Celovec), Marburg (Maribor), Radkersburg (Radgona) and Villach (Beljak) – fell within the predominantly Slovene-speaking area the Yugoslavs demanded.

Second, population estimates by the two sides differed signif-icantly. Austrians contested Yugoslav figures, which showed a clear Slav majority, with 426,000 Slovenes and 78,000 Aus-trians in Styria and 124,000 Slovenes and 38,000 Austrians in Carinthia.[24] As elsewhere, the Yugoslav delegation backed its claims with cultural-historical and economic arguments. South Slav nationalism had significant appeal in Lower Styria and Carinthia in the 19th century, and the regions had long had close ties with the rest of 'Slovenia'. Carinthia in particu-lar was seen as vital for Yugoslavia's economy, since main railways connecting Istria and central Europe ran through the region.

The claims in Austria posed two problems for the Yugo-slavs. The first one was internal: a Slovene-Serb united front appeared to be emerging against the Croats, who maintained their belief in the strict adherence to the nationality prin-ciple. The second was external: Yugoslav claims in Austria were regarded by the Allies as excessive,[25] while the Yugoslavs objected to the minorities provision the Austrian Treaty con-tained, initially refusing to sign it. The dispute over the Kla-genfurt region would be settled by a referendum in October 1920.

7

War Crimes and War Guilt

The Serb-Croat-Slovene delegation was concerned not only with its territorial claims, but also with wider issues related to the legacy of the war and the post-war order. Its members took part in the work of the Reparations Commission and were involved in negotiations over the former Austro-Hungarian fleet. As a member of the League of Nations Commission, Vesnić worked on the Covenant of the League of Nations, of which the Kingdom of Serbs, Croats and Slovenes was a founding member (the League of Nations, enumerated in President Wilson's Fourteen Points, came into being during the Peace Conference). At the final session of the Commission, held on 11 April 1919, Vesnić voted in favour of a Japanese amendment on racial equality, which Wilson opposed.[1]

Representatives of Yugoslavia in Paris saw the future of their country tied to the democratic Allies, the USA, Britain and France. Yugoslavia was, in their view, a natural member of the new international order that would be based on democracy, freedom and justice, as the *Memorandum on Claims* explicitly stated.[2] In a lecture given in Belgrade in January 1920, Vesnić interpreted the First World War as being a struggle between freedom and tyranny – very much echoing the Allied discourse – and welcomed its outcome as a representative of a victorious nation (Serbs) which contributed to the victory 'with its best blood'. The war's outcome was also to be welcomed because it had finally brought about the liberation of Serbs, Croats and Slovenes and given them an opportunity to form a unified state. 'I am absolutely certain [Yugoslavia] will be a worthy member of the new international community as shall be represented by the League of Nations', Vesnić stated. He then admitted that ideally the League should have included the defeated countries, 'but we had to take into account facts in front of us, chief among them the mood among the peoples and public opinion [in the countries which had been victims of the aggression], with horrific war events still fresh in memory'.[3]

Responsibility for the war

The First World War saw great civilian suffering, and the idea that those responsible for war crimes should be tried had emerged before the war was over. Western leaders were preoccupied with the question of German guilt and the punishment of Germany's leadership. Lloyd George allegedly wanted Kaiser Wilhelm II shot, an idea rejected as too radical by Winston Churchill and Lord Curzon. In late November 1918, Britain sought the extradition and trial of the Kaiser (much to the chagrin of the Kaiser's cousin King George V), but the Netherlands, where he had sought refuge, refused to hand him over. Exactly a week after the Peace Conference had begun, the Commission on the Responsibility of the Authors of the War and the Enforcement of Penalties (hereafter, Commission on Responsibility) was established. It argued that responsibility for the war rested firstly with

Germany and Austria, secondly with Bulgaria and Turkey. However, Robert Lansing, US Secretary of State and chairman of the Commission, believed that there was no basis in international law for the Kaiser's prosecution. On Wilson's instructions, Lansing issued a report accepting the right of Allied countries to try, either individually or jointly, by military tribunals individuals accused of violating the laws and customs of war. The report, however, denied their right to establish an international tribunal to try a head of state.[4] The story of German war guilt and Article 231 of the Versailles Treaty (which places the blame for war chiefly on Germany) is a well-known one and is dealt with elsewhere.[5]

The Allied Powers – even the Italians – thought that the Austro-Hungarian forces had only committed relatively minor crimes and did not hold Emperor Karl personally responsible for the war. They were also discouraged from pursuing the question of Austro-Hungarian responsibility due to the complexity of the matter. The Dual Monarchy had disintegrated and in its place several countries had emerged, some formed by Allied nations. The Austrian delegation in Paris exploited the situation and the mood among the Allies. 'What if two officers of the same regiment of the Austro-Hungarian army – one an Austrian-German, the other a Czech – were accused of the same crime? The Austrian would have to be surrendered, while the Czech would not', the Austrians pointed out. In any case, the Allies considered the question of German guilt the most important one, and did not wish to waste much time with a complex case of a state that no longer existed. As for other former enemy states, the Allies regarded the Turks as major culprits, but were not too interested in alleged Bulgarian atrocities.[6]

Punishing Bulgaria

Territories that made up the Kingdom of Serbs, Croats and Slovenes were severely affected by the war. In addition to a largely destroyed infrastructure and a crippled economy, human losses were extremely high. Serbia alone may have lost up to one million people during the war – nearly 370,000 soldiers (more than half of those mobilised) and some 600,000 civilians, many of whom had died of disease or hunger, but also many killed during the fighting and occupation. The South Slavs in Austria-Hungary had lost some 300,000 soldiers, the majority of them being Croats.[7]

The Yugoslav delegation in Paris singled out Bulgarian occupation troops for their brutality. While the Allies, and the French in particular, sought to place the blame for war largely on Germany and the Kaiser, the Yugoslavs were mostly interested in the guilt of Bulgaria and its King Ferdinand. If in Western eyes Germany had been the chief aggressor, Bulgaria was its Balkan equivalent in the Serb-Yugoslav view. The Yugoslavs blamed Bulgaria for aggression against Serbia in 1913 and in 1915, and for atrocities its soldiers committed during the Second Balkan War and the First World War. Indeed, Yugoslavia's territorial claims in and general attitude towards Bulgaria were closely connected with the question of Bulgarian war guilt and punishment of Bulgarian nationals held responsible for war crimes committed in occupied Serbia.

Interestingly, the Yugoslavs did not particularly insist on Austria-Hungary's guilt for the war or for atrocities its soldiers committed in occupied Serbia and Montenegro. So long as a Habsburg restoration was not going to happen, they were happy to forget about their late principal nemesis.[8] Unlike Austria-Hungary, Bulgaria, although defeated, was still around, and Pašić in particular sought to neutralise

Sofia's ability to wage future wars on its western neighbour. In addition, raising the question of war crimes committed by Austria-Hungary's soldiers could have triggered some difficult questions about atrocities committed by the South Slavs serving in the Emperor's army. General Stjepan Sarkotić, an ethnic Croat and wartime military governor of Bosnia-Herzegovina, was responsible for the arrest, forced labour, imprisonment and murder of thousands of Serbs, while mostly Croat and Muslim *Schutzcorps* ('defence forces') had massacred and forcibly expelled Serb villagers from eastern Bosnia.[9] There were also many Habsburg Serbs who had fought against the Serbian army.

During the war, Pašić's government had already established its own commission to investigate war crimes committed by Austrian, Bulgarian and German occupation troops. In order to ensure a fair investigation, the government appointed three foreign experts to the commission (a Briton, a Frenchman, and Dr Archibald Reiss, a Swiss who would be a member of the International Law Section of the Serb-Croat-Slovene delegation in Paris, headed by Slobodan Jovanović). The material the commission prepared was brought to Paris by Jovanović and used to raise charges against 500 Bulgarian nationals, including King Ferdinand himself. Eventually, the Yugoslavs singled out twenty-five chief perpetrators and demanded their extradition to Yugoslavia even before a peace treaty with Bulgaria had been signed in November 1919.

The Yugoslavs – Pašić and Jovanović in particular – closely followed the work of the Commission on Responsibility. They also discussed two wider, related questions debated among the Allies in Paris: could a head of state be tried for war crimes, and with whom should responsibility for crimes lie – individuals, including heads of state, or whole nations?

Pašić was against bringing King Ferdinand to trial. Doing so, in his view, would effectively place all the blame on the Bulgarian monarch and absolve Bulgaria's political leadership and people of all guilt. As Pašić explained during the meeting of the delegation held on 12 February, *responsibility for war should not be placed on individuals, rulers, [because] that would minimize the responsibility of the [Bulgarian] people.* In other words, Pašić argued, *Ferdinand's responsibility must not be used to hide the responsibility of the Bulgarian people ... the whole Bulgarian nation is responsible for the war on Serbia, as is Ferdinand.* The delegates expressed their agreement with Pašić's explanation.[10]

'If one had opened his heart, one would have found these three words inscribed in it: Serbia, Bulgaria, Albania. With hatred, Bulgaria; with greediness, Albania; but Serbia, his little peasant Serbia, with boundless love and pride.'

CARLO SFORZA ON PAŠIĆ[11]

Pašić's view was based on the argument that neither Kaiser Wilhelm nor King Ferdinand could have waged such a long and exhausting war without the support of their people as a whole. No one in the Bulgarian parliament had protested against the war, according to the head of the Yugoslav delegation, while ordinary soldiers had committed atrocities, often long after military operations were over. If King Ferdinand were to be charged and found guilty, he could be used as a scapegoat by the Bulgarian nation, explained Pašić.

His argument was flawed in one respect at least: not all Bulgarians had supported the war. Most famously, Aleksandŭr Stamboliĭski, leader of Bulgarian Agrarians, had been imprisoned for his public criticism of it. In fact, Stamboliĭski would be appointed Prime Minister at the end of the war and sent to the Peace Conference to negotiate peace terms with the Allies, largely because of his well-known anti-war record. Pašić, of course, had been aware of this. After the Bulgarian delegation arrived in Paris on 24 October 1919 to sign the peace treaty, Stamboliĭski, as head of the delegation, wrote to his Greek, Romanian and Yugoslav counterparts, reassuring them of Bulgaria's commitment to peace in the Balkans and reminding them of his own opposition to the war.[12] The Balkan leaders, unfortunately, refused to shake the extended hand of the new Bulgarian leader. The Allies seemed just as unimpressed: Stamboliĭski and the rest of the Bulgarian delegation were kept outside Paris and were explicitly forbidden from coming to the city unless invited by the Conference.

It was Slobodan Jovanović, an expert on international law, who lent scholarly authority to Pašić's arguments. Jovanović, too, argued that responsibility for the war lay with the Bulgarian people, not just its leadership. He believed the problem should be internationalised, and proposed the setting up of an international criminal court for war crimes committed by Bulgarian nationals.

While Trumbić and other non-Serb members of the delegation largely stayed out of the debate – as if it were purely a Serb-Bulgarian matter – Bošković entered into an argument with Pašić and Jovanović. Bošković thought the peace treaty with Bulgaria ought to single out King Ferdinand's responsibility, just as the German treaty singled out the Kaiser's responsibility. Because neither Pašić nor Bošković would compromise their views, the matter was referred to the government in Belgrade. Prime Minister Protić replied that the two views actually complemented each other: both the Bulgarian leadership, including Ferdinand, and ordinary Bulgarians were guilty. Pašić, in the meanwhile, sought to secure support from his Greek and Romanian counterparts for placing collective blame on the Bulgarian nation.[13]

With Jovanović's help, the Greeks and the Romanians agreed to the proposal for the establishment of an inter-Allied court that would deal with Bulgarian war crimes and establish the extent of the country's guilt for the war. The proposal was formally submitted to the Commission on Responsibility on 15 July 1919. The Balkan representatives also stated that their countries would not seek Ferdinand's trial. The British were sympathetic, and thought the 'Serbian' [sic] proposal fair, but it was ultimately rejected due to French opposition. The French were concerned that such a tribunal would set a precedent that might encourage the Germans to seek to revise the Versailles Treaty. The Treaty explicitly stipulated that German citizens responsible for war crimes would be tried by courts of the country that brought charges against them – in other words, France.

The following month, the Yugoslavs (most probably Jovanović) drafted a memorandum on Bulgarian guilt, to be submitted to the Big Four by Yugoslavia, Greece and Romania. The memorandum stated that the magnitude of Bulgarian crimes deserved to be condemned by the whole world. Moreover, sentences issued by an international court would contribute to pacification and reconciliation in the region. The Bulgarians were more likely to accept and take seriously such a body, rather than the courts of their neighbours. The document made a direct parallel between Germany and Bulgaria: the victorious Balkan states should treat the latter the same way the Allies treated the former, as that was the only way to ensure that Bulgarians fulfilled the conditions to be set out in the future peace treaty. The Bulgarian Treaty, the Yugoslav memorandum stated, should include a clause making it compulsory for Bulgaria to hand over its citizens accused of war crimes by other countries. In the end, the memorandum was never submitted because the Greeks produced a similar note which the Yugoslavs accepted. However, neither Yugoslav nor Greek efforts to establish an international court for Bulgarian citizens was going to succeed in persuading the Allies to support it.[14]

Ironically, Stamboliĭski's Bulgaria did more than most other countries to punish those responsible for war crimes, partly because the Bulgarian leader was keen to establish friendly relations with Yugoslavia and other Balkan states. While King Ferdinand emigrated to Germany, where his hosts protected him, several wartime ministers were tried. A Bulgarian army major was tried and executed for ordering a massacre of Serb civilians in Niš.[15] Stamboliĭski would in the end pay a heavy price for his attempts to break with the past so radically. The Bulgarian government would be overthrown in a nationalist *coup d'état* in June 1923 and the Prime Minister brutally murdered by his domestic opponents.

8

The Adriatic Question

It was the Adriatic question which dominated the Yugoslav agenda in Paris, certainly during the first six months of the Conference. The Yugoslav delegation met on an almost daily basis, sometimes twice-daily. Pašić, who rarely left his hotel, normally called the meetings. He would usually start by summarising the previous meeting, often giving his own version of events, which did not always correspond to what had really taken place. Following what was usually a long monologue, delivered slowly, Pašić would let others speak, preferring to listen and keep his views to himself. When differences within the delegation arose, the delegates often wondered what Pašić thought – sometimes, they had to wait until the following meeting and his 'summary' to find out. Such behaviour infuriated others, especially Trumbić and Smodlaka.[1]

It seemed as if Trumbić's position on the Adriatic question – that national self-determination should be the guiding principle – was gathering support from outside the Political Section. On 26 January, Pašić read out a telegram from the government concerning the border with Italy. The message was simple: 'Stick to the principle of nationality as far as possible.' There was also a message from Professor Cvijić, who, possibly anxious that the experts' opinion would not be sought by the politicians, asked the delegates to consult the Ethnographic Section before submitting the memorandum on claims.[2]

Two days later, Trumbić suddenly proposed a radical solution to the Adriatic problem: demilitarisation of the coast and the islands. Such a solution would be in Yugoslavia's best interests, Trumbić argued. It would take away Italy's argument that it needed Istria and Dalmatia for security reasons; it would place Yugoslavia on an equal footing with Italy, otherwise a far superior naval power; it would protect Yugoslavia from its aggressive western neighbour; and it would lead to significant savings of money that would have gone into defending such a long coast. Apart from Smodlaka, no one supported the proposal. Vesnić argued that it would limit the country's sovereignty and weaken its international standing, politically as well as 'morally'. Since no consensus could be found, Pašić and Ribarž suggested that the proposal should be sent to Belgrade, but refused to recommend it to the government.[3] This meant its chances of success were slim from the start. It also meant that potentially the first real opportunity for the Yugoslav delegation to break the ice in the Adriatic was lost.

Wilson's role

Britain and France were sympathetic to the Yugoslavs' claims in the Adriatic, but were bound by the Treaty of London. Both Paris and London hoped that Belgrade and Rome would find a compromise solution; a solution that would also mean a compromise between America's insistence on national self-determination and the legacy of wartime secret diplomacy.

President Wilson's famously strong views in favour of national self-determination and his rejection of secret treaties promised to give the Yugoslavs a powerful ally in Paris. Before the American entry into the war in April 1917, the US President had expressed little interest in the Balkans and knew next to nothing about the movement for South Slav unification. In this he was not alone among the Allied statesmen. When Lloyd George and Pašić met for the first time in October 1918, the British Prime Minister asked whether Serbs and Croats spoke the same language.[4] However, once the US entered the war, things changed. In the summer of 1917, a group of experts working under the supervision of Colonel Edward M House, President Wilson's right-hand man (and later one of the key members of the US delegation in Paris), began to prepare material for a future peace conference, and US policy towards the small nations of East-Central Europe began to take shape. The Inquiry – as the group of experts became known – supported the right of each nation to self-determination, but did not advocate the dissolution of Austria-Hungary. Only in the final stages of the war, when the dismemberment of the Dual Monarchy seemed inevitable, would they begin explicitly to support a Yugoslav union. The 'Yugoslav' experts within the Inquiry, who included the academics Robert Kerner, Dana Munro and Charles Seymour, argued that the unification of the Yugoslavs was consistent with the Wilsonian principle of national self-determination, and that the South Slav union was essential for peace and stability in East-Central Europe.[5] The experts rejected the Treaty of London as a dangerous document that would sow the seeds of a future war. Colonel House told Orlando as much when they met in Paris in early January 1919.

On 21 January 1919 the Inquiry produced a report which

rejected the Treaty of London and effectively recommended the recognition of Yugoslavia. The report supported an independent South Slav *federation*, comprising Serbia, Montenegro and the South Slav provinces of former Austria-Hungary. It proposed a compromise solution, based roughly on linguistic boundaries, for borders between the Yugoslav state and Austria, Hungary and Romania. It called for a partition of Istria between Italy and Yugoslavia, with eastern parts going to the latter, and proposed that Yugoslavia receive Fiume and Dalmatia. The old Serbian borders with Bulgaria, Greece and Romania should be preserved. As for the border with Albania, the report recommended that Yugoslavia should be given northern Albania, as a 'reward' for Serbia's contribution to the Allied victory.

The report would decisively inform Wilson's view of the Yugoslav union in general and the Yugoslav-Italian dispute in particular.[6] At the Peace Conference, President Wilson and the American delegation generally would prove to be a major Yugoslav ally. However, Wilson's attempt to break the Yugoslav-Italian deadlock in Paris hit a serious obstacle right from the start. The Italians and Romanians had made a pact to stick to the secret treaties. The Italians told the Americans to stay out of European business. Sonnino even made a dramatic declaration that if the Treaty of London were broken, Italy would start preparing for war and would defend itself against the Franco-Serbian alliance.[7]

On 2 February, Stéphen Pichon, the French Foreign Minister, suddenly invited the Yugoslavs to visit him, without giving precise reasons for the invitation. Pašić, Trumbić and Vesnić went, believing they would discuss the Banat issue, as they had done three days previously at the Council of Ten. Instead, Pichon wanted to talk about the dispute with Italy in the Adriatic. He explained that France, as well as Britain, while sympathetic to the Yugoslav cause, was bound by the Treaty of London. Therefore, he wondered whether the Yugoslavs might try harder to reach a compromise with Italy.

Trumbić came out of the meeting convinced that the delegation should ask Wilson to mediate between them and Italy. He made the proposal in front of the full delegation, which had convened at the Hotel Beau-Site after the meeting with Pichon. The proposal surprised the other delegates as it seemed to have come out of the blue, but they liked it. Trumbić has sometimes been credited with initiating Wilson's arbitration in the Yugoslav-Italian dispute; in reality, however, the suggestion effectively came from the Americans. It had in fact been initiated the previous day, when Trumbić met Lansing. The leading member of the American delegation had invited his Yugoslav counterpart to talk about recent South Slav history, politics and their future plans. Trumbić raised the question of recognition of the Serb-Croat-Slovene Kingdom by Washington. The American would not promise anything, but Trumbić correctly sensed that the US delegation was favourably disposed to his country. He was given a clear impression that President Wilson was keen to settle the Adriatic question before his scheduled, temporary return to the US, in order to deal with matters of domestic politics (Wilson would leave Paris on 14 February, almost immediately following his presentation of the draft Covenant of the League of Nations, and would return a month later).[9]

> 'My God, my God! Italy or Yugoslavia? The blonde or the brunette?'
>
> CLEMENCEAU'S DILEMMA[8]

Events now moved in quick succession. On 6 February, Trumbić met Wilson and once again presented the Yugoslav position on the Adriatic dispute. At the same time, the delegation received news from Belgrade that the government accepted the proposal to ask the US President to arbitrate in the Italo-Yugoslav dispute, but, as was expected, rejected Trumbić's other proposal, for the neutralisation of the Adriatic. On 11 February, Pašić, Trumbić, Vesnić and Žolger formally requested Wilson's arbitration in a short letter, twice mentioning the full name of the delegation:

'Mr. President,
Inspired by the fullest confidence in the lofty spirit of justice which you have displayed in regard to all questions appertaining to the Peace Settlement, and desirous of contributing to the friendly solution of the territorial differences pending between the Kingdom of Serbs, Croats and Slovenes and the Kingdom of Italy, the Delegation of the Kingdom of Serbs, Croats and Slovenes desires to bring to your knowledge its readiness to submit those differences to your arbitration. It has received full authority to this effect from its Government. With the assurance of our profound esteem, we are, Mr. President,
    Respectfully,
    Pachitch – Trumbić – Vesnitch – Žolger
                The Delegation of the Kingdom of Serbs,
                                Croats and Slovenes'[10]

Unbeknown to the Yugoslavs, the Italians had presented their territorial claims to the Council of Ten four days previously. In addition to territories promised by the Treaty of London, they now demanded Fiume as well. By doing so they weakened their position in two ways. Firstly, by asking for Fiume they contradicted their unrepentant insistence on the implementation of the Treaty of London. Secondly, they annoyed Wilson to the extent that he was now firmly in the pro-Yugoslav camp. On the very same day, 7 February 1919, the US officially recognised the Kingdom of Serbs, Croats and Slovenes. The Americans stopped short of recognising the Yugoslav character of the Belgrade delegation, but the recognition of the country, the first by a major power, was nevertheless a *coup* for Belgrade. Trumbić's meeting with Wilson the previous day had clearly made a positive impression on the President, but the Italians' lack of tact influenced his decision, too.

The Yugoslavs were aware that much hard work remained to be done and that their position, notwithstanding the American recognition of the state, remained precarious. In the wake of American recognition, Trumbić wrote to Belgrade to express his satisfaction with the government's support of his proposal to ask for Wilson's arbitration. He added that the French and British liked the idea as well. However, [*t*]*he general situation* [*in Paris*] *is not satisfactory. During the whole month nothing has been settled. The conference moves too slowly ... the general feeling is that too much time is given to frontier questions instead of making preliminary peace with Germany. Hence the Powers have decided to concentrate on that and postpone frontier matters for the time being. This is justified from the general point of view but is dangerous for us. The Italian army would remain where it is. Hence the arbitration proposal is all the more important ... I hear the Italians are opposed to the proposal but will be forced to accept it.*[11] As it turned out, Orlando rejected the proposal for US arbitration, but the Yugoslavs were not to know this for another few weeks.

At 11.00 a.m. on 18 February Pašić informed the delegation that it was to appear before the Council of Ten at 3.00 p.m. the same day.[12] This would be only the second time the delegation had appeared before the Council since the Conference had begun exactly one month previously. Just as when the Yugoslavs were invited by the Council the first time, on 31 January, the invitation was sent at extremely short notice, and once again they were not informed of the agenda. They did not know whether they should be prepared to discuss the Adriatic question only, or all their territorial claims.

Vesnić spoke for the delegation when he expressed his bitterness at being kept in the dark for so long by the Conference. Trumbić suggested a formal protest should be lodged, because Italy, a member of the Council of Ten, clearly could not be neutral and should not be treated as a member of the Council when Yugoslav claims were discussed. Pašić thought that expressing dissatisfaction openly, however justified, would risk alienating the Allies. He persuaded Trumbić that an official complaint would be counterproductive. The delegates agreed they should make a more discreet point about the importance of the Yugoslavs and Italians being treated equally. This episode perfectly illustrates Pašić's belief in always working *with* the Allies – or at least giving them this impression – and Trumbić's less measured approach.

Although in comparison with the delegations of the defeated countries the Yugoslavs were dealt with courteously by the Supreme Council, their feeling of dissatisfaction with their treatment is understandable. It was also probably mixed with a sense of apprehension caused by the temporary absence from Paris of President Wilson, their most powerful supporter, who had left for the US four days previously.

At 3.00 p.m., Pašić, Trumbić, Vesnić and Žolger appeared in front of the Council of Ten in Pichon's office at the Quai d'Orsay. Vesnić, the most capable speaker among the Yugoslavs, spoke first, starting with an apology for not supplying the Council in advance with a full memorandum on the claims, due to difficulties caused by distance and poor communications with Belgrade. He explained that a general memorandum had been prepared and that more detailed appendices would follow. He then provided an overview of Yugoslav claims, ending by expressing his confidence that the Council would treat the Yugoslavs and the Italians equally in matters concerning both delegations. While Vesnić was describing claims on Bulgaria, Clemenceau whispered to him that those would be obtained without great difficulty. Trumbić then took the floor, with a lengthy presentation on frontiers with Italy, followed by Žolger's presentation of claims in the north and the importance of Yugoslavia as a bulwark against pan-Germanism. Pašić did not speak.[13]

The memorandum to which Vesnić referred was an eleven-page document, with two maps showing Yugoslav 'ethnographic' territory appended. It stated that '[t]he Serbians, Croatians and Slovenes constitute one single nation' and that 'the Kingdom of the Serbians, Croatians and Slovenes is an accomplished fact, resulting from the will of the people', before adding that governments of the Allied and neutral countries had been notified of the unification. It then listed briefly the territories which the Yugoslavs claimed, but without going into a detailed description – was this because there was still no internal agreement within the delegation regarding the matter? The memorandum emphasised several times that national self-determination was Yugoslavia's *raison d'étre* and the guiding principle behind its territorial demands. It claimed that the Yugoslav union was in the interest of the new international order being created in Paris, and praised the role of the Allies, but especially the United States, in the war, which had finally brought about South Slav liberation.[14]

After the Yugoslavs had left the room, members of the Council discussed the claims of the delegation of the 'Kingdom of Serbia'. Lloyd George thought the Yugoslavs presented an 'exceedingly able statement', while the Americans felt it was a rather 'long and dull presentation'. Orlando and Sonnino persuaded their counterparts that the dispute in the eastern Adriatic was to be settled by the Council, while all other Yugoslav claims would be dealt with by separate territorial commissions. The Italians thus pushed the Council into adopting a double standard, an act without parallel at the Conference.[15]

Understandably, the government in Belgrade was furious. Prime Minister Protić cabled Trumbić on 23 February, stating that: 'The Cabinet cannot understand the inconsistency of the powers ... [it] feels there can be only one course between these two: either France, England [sic] and Italy should give up the London Treaty and then the conference can freely resolve the dispute ... or, accept our proposal for American arbitration. If neither is accepted, the Cabinet will seriously have to consider whether there is any sense in our participating in the conference.'[16]

In a cable to Pašić, sent three days later, Protić complained that 'we cannot agree that the Conference resolves our dispute while the Treaty of London remains in force, for that would mean that the litigants would act as judges'. Trumbić replied to Protić that *things have not yet come to the point of our leaving the peace conference*, adding that Wilson's refusal to recognise the Treaty of London *is our only hope*. Italy had resolutely rejected American arbitration the day before the Council received the Yugoslav delegation, but the Yugoslavs only found out on 3 March, when Clemenceau suddenly informed them of the fact.[17]

> **MEMORANDUM PRESENTED TO THE PEACE CONFERENCE, IN PARIS, CONCERNING THE CLAIMS OF THE KINGDOM OF THE SERBIANS, CROATIANS AND SLOVENES**
>
> The Serbians, Croatians and Slovenes constitute one single nation which possesses, already very long, her particular civilization and her intellectual unity. [...] Thus the Kingdom of the Serbians, Croatians and Slovenes is an accomplished fact, resulting from the will of the people. [...] The regions inhabited by our nation comprise the territories situated in the Southern Alps, on the banks of the Sotcha, the Mur, the Drave, the Save, the Danube, the Tisza, the Timok, the Vardar and the Strouma, and on the coast of the Adriatic Sea. Our people possesses a very developed conscience of its national unity. The territories which it occupies present quite a particular importance from the point of view of European interests, because of their geographical situation. They connect Central Europe with the Near-East, the Mediterranean and Asia Minor. During the five last centuries, bloody wars have been fought, nearly without interruption, for the possession of these regions, between two great Empires, Austria and Turkey; both of these Empires have disappeared. [...]
>
> It is absolutely necessary for the future peace that normal conditions of existence be finally secured to this important part of Europe; this can only be done by the creation of a single State, based on the principle of nationalities. The general interests demand that all the possibilities of a regular existence be secured to this State; only in this way will it be able to consolidate itself and to devote all its energies to its economical [*sic*] and intellectual development. And this can only be done if our people,

The Yugoslavs had little choice but to stand aside and let the Americans force the Italians to compromise. This was a wise tactic: the British and the French harboured the same hope – that Wilson would force Orlando's hand – because they were bound by the terms of the Treaty of London, which, between themselves, they wished the Italians would stop insisting upon so unrepentantly.

On 14 March Wilson returned to Paris, to be presented with the Italian memorandum, which claimed the territories promised by the Treaty of London as well as Fiume. Despite divisions within the American delegation over the matter which has conquered its independence, completely resolves the problem of its State frontiers in such a way that they unite all the people belonging to the race of the Serbians, Croatians and Slovenes.

The principle of nationalities imposes this solution as [an] essential condition of the new state of things which has to be created in the Peace Conference. [...]

In consequence, we demand the recognition of the union to our State of all countries which, according to the principle of nationalities, must belong to it.

Our claims are therefore just, moral and liberal; they are equally inspired by the principles solemnly proclaimed by the allied and associated States as principles which must constitute the base of the new order of things in Europe.

No European nation has saluted with more joy the principles in the name of which our Allies and the United States of America have fought this world's war, than our nation, which, during centuries, has not ceased to fight for the guarantee of its national liberties and its existence.

Thanks to the valour and the spirit of self-denial of our powerful Allies and the United States of America, after atrocious losses and devastations, victory remained in the hands of those who rose for the defence of Justice and of human civilization.

The representatives of the Kingdom of the Serbians, Croatians and Slovenes beg the Peace Conference to equitably examine their claims and to adopt them.

– some high-ranking members of the American delegation unsuccessfully proposed that most Italian claims be accepted – Wilson was determined Italy should not receive Fiume. In this he was supported by Lloyd George and Clemenceau.

The Allies may had been sympathetic to the Yugoslavs, but at the same time they ignored public protestations by Prince Regent Alexander, the Belgrade government and its delegation in Paris over Italy's claims, and their repeated calls for the Treaty of London to be declared invalid. For instance, Pašić unsuccessfully appealed, in a letter to Clemenceau of 31 March, that the Allies stop treating the

Yugoslav provinces formerly of the Habsburg Monarchy as enemy territory.[18]

The same day Pašić sent his letter, a surprising development occurred during a meeting of the delegation. In addition to competing for territory, Belgrade and Rome were also involved in difficult negotiations over the former Austro-Hungarian fleet. Božo Banac, a member of the Yugoslav Naval Section, who attended the meeting together with three other maritime experts, reported that he had been approached by an Italian counterpart with a view to settling the issue of the fleet. The Italian view was not unreasonable: unless the two sides settled the problem quickly and directly, the British and the French were likely to receive a share of the fleet. The Italian told Banac that his delegation's motto was 'the Adriatic for the Adriatic nations'. Despite some concern within the delegation, mainly by the Serb members who believed they should not deal with the Italians without consulting the Allies, it was decided, after a long debate, that the possibility of a settlement should be explored. The delegation rightly concluded that were the traditional naval powers to divide the fleet, the Yugoslavs could end up not obtaining anything, since only 'Serbia', a landlocked country, was formally accepted by the Conference. The delegation also accepted Banac's proposal that the preliminary contacts be raised to a political level; Trumbić was to meet with Silvio Crespi, a high-ranking Italian delegate, and discuss the matter.[19]

'It [Yugoslavia] will be a turbulent nation, as they are a turbulent people, and they ought not to have a navy to run amuck with.'

WOODROW WILSON[20]

Although it offered genuine promise, the meeting between Trumbić and Crespi of 11 April turned out to be a failure.

Instead of discussing the fleet issue, Crespi began by telling Trumbić that the Yugoslavs would never get Fiume, and that it was therefore better for them to give it up in exchange for Italy's recognition of the Serb-Croat-Slovene state and economic concessions in the Adriatic. Trumbić categorically rejected the suggestion: *I speak here only privately, but I am convinced that my view is shared by my whole nation: Fiume must be ours and about this there can be absolutely no discussion*. The meeting thus ended without this crucial issue being resolved, which could have begun rapprochement between the two sides.[21]

A week before, Trumbić had expressed his and the delegation's position on Fiume in similarly categorical terms. In their typically 'last minute' style, the Big Four (in reality the Big Three, because Orlando, as it turned out, refused to be present) invited someone from the Yugoslav delegation at 1.00 p.m. on 4 April, to appear before the members of the Council at 4.00 p.m. that same day. This time, the Yugoslavs were at least informed of the agenda: one item, the Adriatic question. Trumbić, sent as the most qualified representative, attempted to present, once again, the Yugoslav position on the eastern Adriatic, but Clemenceau, Lloyd George and Wilson interrupted him; they were really only interested in the Fiume question. 'Could Split [Spalato] serve as the major port?', Wilson asked, to which Trumbić replied that only Fiume could serve the purpose. The Yugoslav Foreign Minister returned to the delegation's headquarters with some optimism regarding Fiume: Lloyd George publicly stated his agreement with Trumbić's arguments, while Wilson and Clemenceau, Trumbić believed, were similarly sympathetic.[22]

Wilson maintained the initiative. On 14 April he met Orlando twice to discuss the Adriatic question. He proposed a border largely coinciding with the one stipulated by the Treaty of London, and a partition of Istria. For Fiume, the US President proposed 'free city' status, but under Yugoslav customs authority. The proposal became known as the 'Wilson line'. Orlando rejected it, possibly encouraged by Wilson's seemingly softer stance in respect of the Treaty of London, which he had previously treated as illegitimate.

The Yugoslavs sensed the moment was right to make some moves of their own. On 16 April Trumbić, with Pašić's approval, presented Clemenceau with a proposal for a plebiscite in the entire area claimed by Italy and Yugoslavia; copies of the proposal were sent to Wilson, Lloyd George and Orlando. The following day Pašić went to see Wilson. The President's sympathies for the old Serb statesman were obvious. Pašić presented the Yugoslav claims everywhere, not just in the Adriatic, and pressed the right button by urging the President to support the Yugoslavs' right to national self-determination, even though, privately, he had been a reluctant supporter of the idea. He shrewdly showered the President with compliments, appealing to his ego, and pretended that the Yugoslav delegation was prepared to be moderate regarding Bulgaria. Wilson was won over – and possibly manipulated – by Pašić. Reporting back from the meeting, Pašić, somewhat uncharacteristically, openly expressed his confidence in front of the delegation that Wilson *will help our just claims*. Although the President made no promises, the meeting with Pašić 'no doubt influenced Wilson's whole attitude in the mounting crisis', according to the historian Lederer.[23]

The Italians walk out ... and return

The Yugoslavs were not kept informed of stormy sessions in the Council of Four that were taking place at the time, although they received leaked information from several sources that intense talks were going on. They were as shocked as everyone else when Wilson decided that enough was enough and issued a public memorandum on 23 April, designed to appeal to the Italian nation as well as to the rest of the world. In the memorandum, he proposed the 'Wilson line' of settlement and publicly asked Italy to accept it. This sudden and bold act had the opposite effect from the one intended. The Italian delegation left Paris in protest, and rather than turning the Italians against their Prime Minister, Wilson's move backfired. Orlando's action was endorsed by Italian public opinion, with demonstrations of popular support.

The Yugoslavs reacted moderately to the Italian walkout. They were encouraged by the Italians' undiplomatic reaction, but at the same time remained concerned that after all these months of negotiations a solution to the dispute appeared as remote as ever. They were also worried that the Italians might use the situation to launch a military offensive against Yugoslavia. Trumbić wrote to Clemenceau expressing the delegation's hope that the Allies would intervene on Yugoslavia's behalf in the event of an Italian attack, and proposed to Protić that the Belgrade parliament send an appeal to the American Congress for support against a possible invasion by Italy.[24]

Orlando and Sonnino returned to Paris on 7 May, the same day the draft of the German Treaty was presented. They did so because the British and the French threatened, in the event of a prolonged Italian boycott of the Conference, to declare that they were no longer bound by the terms of the Treaty of London. The Italians now made a concession by agreeing to accept 'free city' status for Fiume. However, an agreement remained elusive. The Yugoslavs were suspicious – correctly as it turned out – that the city would be *de facto* under Italian control. While the Yugoslavs mistrusted the Italians, the Italian delegates refused to meet members of the Yugoslav delegation officially, lest it be interpreted as *de facto* recognition of the Serb-Croat-Slovene Kingdom. Thus, following the Italians' return to Paris, Orlando and Trumbić 'met' in a Parisian hotel, but remained in separate rooms, with Colonel House acting as go-between.[25]

Towards a settlement

On 19 June 1919, Orlando lost the parliamentary elections at home. Francesco Nitti became the new Prime Minister, while Tommaso Tittoni replaced Sonnino as Foreign Minister. However, little changed in respect of the Adriatic crisis. When the Versailles Treaty was signed on 28 June, the question of the Italo-Yugoslav border still remained open. Wilson left Paris, satisfied that with the signing of the 'German Treaty' the main job was done, but disappointed he had not been able to resolve the Adriatic dispute.

For the Yugoslavs there was some consolation that by signing the Versailles Treaty as the delegation of the Kingdom of Serbs, Croats and Slovenes, their country was at last recognised by all the Allies, including Italy. The attention of the peacemakers now turned to a treaty with Austria, which would be concluded at St Germain on 10 September 1919 – but initially without a Yugoslav signature. Two days later, on 12 September, Gabrielle D'Annunzio, an Italian poet and a nationalist, raised a small force and invaded Fiume. The act was condemned by the Yugoslavs as well as the Allies, but the occupation continued.

As did increasingly hopeless negotiations between Italy and

Yugoslavia. In the autumn of 1919, Italy expressed willingness to reduce its aims in Dalmatia. However, Fiume continued to be a stumbling block. Later that year Tittoni resigned in frustration, but his successor Vittorio Scialoja proved just as unsuccessful, despite offering further concessions in Dalmatia – Italy's demands were now essentially reduced to the city of Zara and several islands. Negotiations continued into the following year, but it became evident that the Italo-Yugoslav border dispute could not be resolved in Paris, even after the French and British had issued an ultimatum to the Yugoslavs in January 1920: either sign a deal with Italy, or the Treaty of London will be implemented.

In June 1920, Giovanni Giolitti formed a new government in Italy and began a renewed initiative to settle the Adriatic dispute. The Yugoslavs, dispirited by America's increasing preoccupation with its internal affairs, and growing Franco-British impatience, accepted Foreign Minister Carlo Sforza's proposal to convene a separate conference outside Paris to deal exclusively with the Adriatic problem. In November 1920, Trumbić went to Rapallo, in north-west Italy, to negotiate a settlement at last. In effect he, and the new Yugoslav government led by Vesnić, were forced to accept the terms of a treaty that was less favourable than Wilson's proposal of April 1919 or the Anglo-French one of January 1920. Trumbić returned home with mixed feelings. He was not happy with the outcome of the settlement, but felt that not signing the Treaty would have eventually resulted in an even less favourable outcome for Yugoslavia, and would have further damaged its relations with Italy. He received a hero's welcome upon returning to his native Split, where in December he gave a public talk on the Adriatic question in a packed theatre.[26]

The Yugoslavs received most of Dalmatia, except for Zara

and four major islands in the eastern Adriatic; Istria went to Italy and Fiume became a 'free state'. The following month, Italian troops expelled D'Annunzio's men, but Fiume was only *de facto* independent. In 1924 Benito Mussolini brought it under formal Italian control. The Yugoslav government – now led by Pašić – had little choice but to accept the annexation, in exchange for some economic concessions. Trumbić, by this time an opposition politician without much popular support, was even more helpless than his old Serbian ally and rival.

9
Settlements

In total, five peace treaties were signed in and around Paris during the Conference. A peace treaty between the Allied and Associated Powers and Germany was signed at Versailles on 28 June 1919. It was followed by the Treaty of St Germain-en-Laye of 10 September 1919 with Austria. On 27 November 1919 a treaty with Bulgaria was signed at Neuilly-sur-Seine. In 1920, treaties with two remaining former enemies were signed: with Hungary on 4 June at Trianon, and with the Ottoman Empire on 10 August, at Sèvres. The Yugoslavs were not invited to sign the last treaty (which would be superseded by the Treaty of Lausanne of 1923), because Serbia and the Ottoman Empire had not been at war.

The two main goals of the Serb-Croat-Slovene delegation in Paris were closely interconnected: achieving territorial claims and internationally-recognised borders. The Treaty of Versailles did not concern Yugoslavia's territorial demands – Germany and the South Slav kingdom shared no borders – but it was the first major international document signed by representatives of the new state. Therefore, the German Treaty meant the *ipso facto* recognition of the Kingdom of

Serbs, Croats and Slovenes, hitherto formally represented by Serbia; with the Versailles Treaty, Serbia – and Montenegro – finally became history (to reappear as independent states in 2006).

The Yugoslav delegates did not sign the Austrian Treaty until early December, due to their initial objection to a controversial article on minority rights. The Yugoslavs felt Article 59 should not concern Serbia, which was neither a defeated country nor a Habsburg successor state, but in the end bowed under pressure from the Allies. If the Treaty of St Germain meant the Allies regarded the Serb-Croat-Slovene Kingdom as a Habsburg successor state, the absence of a Yugoslav signature to the Treaty of Sèvres suggested that Yugoslavia was (also) seen as a successor to the Kingdom of Serbia. Since Serbia had not been at war with the Ottoman Empire during the First World War – the two countries had finished their wars in 1912–13, and were allies in the Second Balkan War of 1913 – there was no need for a Serb-Croat-Slovene signature at Sèvres. The Treaty of Neuilly contained a provision for the protection of minority rights, which the Yugoslavs (and Greeks) signed reluctantly, under Allied pressure.

The attitude of the Allies was not necessarily contradictory. The Kingdom of Serbs, Croats and Slovenes *was* a Habsburg successor state and Serbia's successor state, while half of its territory was made up of formerly enemy lands; therefore, it may be argued that the delegation represented not only victors, but also the defeated. Žolger's presence served as a reminder of this. Ultimately, the reason the Allies insisted the Serb-Croat-Slovene, Greek and Romanian delegations sign the controversial minority provisions was simple: they did not trust the new states of East-Central Europe when it came to the treatment of national minorities.

The Treaty of Versailles

To a contemporary observer it may have seemed as if fate had conspired over the date chosen for the signing of the Versailles Treaty. It was on 28 June that Gavrilo Princip assassinated Franz Ferdinand and Sophie Chotek, an event that sparked the war. It was the anniversary of the 1389 Battle of Kosovo, which inspired the Kosovo myth, central to Serbian and – in the late 19th and early 20th century – Yugoslav nationalist ideology. In retrospect, one may be tempted to claim that the fateful date on which the new state secured international recognition was an ominous sign, just as has been claimed in respect of the 1921 Constitution – promulgated on 28 June – which turned the first Yugoslavia into a Serb-dominated centralised state. It may be argued that it was symbolic that a very harsh peace treaty – not only from the German point of view – was concluded on the anniversary of the Sarajevo assassination, but in reality the date was probably chosen through a combination of coincidence and design.

In late April, the Council of Four asked each delegation to submit the names of those who would sign the treaty with Germany. A seemingly straightforward request exposed problems within the Yugoslav delegation. Vesnić suggested that Pašić, Trumbić and Žolger, as representatives of each Yugoslav 'tribe', should sign the Treaty. However, Žolger refused, lest his signature be interpreted as undermining Slovene demands in Austria (at the time the possibility of the unification of Germany and Austria – the *Anschluss* – had strong popular support in the two countries and could not be discounted, although it seemed unlikely to gain decisive support among the Allies). In the end, Pašić, Trumbić and Vesnić signed the historic Treaty, in the name of 'The Serb-Croat-Slovene State', and as representatives of 'His Majesty

THE POLITICS OF SYMBOLS

The peacemakers certainly had a feel for the symbolic power of historical anniversaries and venues. Probably by design, the Conference opened on 18 January, the anniversary of the 1871 treaty which ended the Franco-Prussian War, with France's defeat and the proclamation of the German Reich, signed in the Hall of Mirrors; the draft German Treaty was presented on 7 May 1919, the fourth anniversary of the sinking of the *Lusitania* by a German U-boat; and Germany signed the humiliating peace treaty in the Hall of Mirrors, on 28 June 1919, the fifth anniversary of the Sarajevo assassination.

In the early hours of 28 June 1940, Adolf Hitler triumphantly toured Paris only days after the French had signed their capitulation in the forest of Compiègne, in Marshal Foch's railway carriage where defeated German generals had signed the armistice on 11 November 1918. It was Hitler who insisted that the old carriage be brought from a museum to the exact spot which symbolised the German humiliation at the end of the First World War. The 1940 Franco-German armistice deliberately mirrored some of the conditions of 1918 and 1919 – for instance, the French army was to be reduced to 100,000 troops.

the King of the Serbs, the Croats, and the Slovenes'. (Žolger would put his signature to the Austrian, Bulgarian and Hungarian Treaties, together with Pašić and Trumbić.)

In early drafts of the German Treaty, the Serb-Croat-Slovene Kingdom was still referred to as 'Serbia', which predictably led to complaints from the Yugoslavs. Faced with the possibility of the Yugoslav delegation refusing to sign the treaty unless its full name was recognised, the Allies finally gave in. The final draft of the Treaty, submitted on 7 May, listed 'Serbie-Croatie-Slavonie' [*sic*] among the Allied and Associated Powers. Trumbić interpreted this to be the act of recognition of the new state by the Conference, at last – even if 'Slovenia' had been clearly confused for 'Slavonia' (a confusion not uncommon outside former Yugoslavia to this day).[1]

After much deliberation, and after securing some minor

concessions, the German delegation accepted the terms of the Treaty at 5.20 p.m. on 24 June, just before the 7.00 p.m. deadline. The terms of the Treaty were infamously harsh – the burden of war guilt was exceeded only by the weight of reparations Germany would have to pay. Once the Germans had bowed under enormous pressure, all delegations were informed that the ceremony of the signing would take place on 28 June, in the Hall of Mirrors at the Palace of Versailles. Both the date and venue were symbolic. Germany would sign the Treaty on the fifth anniversary of the Sarajevo assassination, at the very same place that symbolised French humiliation and the unification of Germany in 1871.[2]

For Britain, France and the United States, the most important task at the Conference was fulfilled with the signing of the Versailles Treaty. Wilson and Lloyd George left Paris soon afterwards. A struggle for borders awaited the delegation of the Kingdom of Serbs, Croats and Slovenes, internationally recognised at least and at last.

The Treaty of St Germain

It was not just the border disputes with Allied Italy and Romania that posed great difficulties for the Serb-Croat-Slovene delegation. The Austrian Treaty would put relations between the Allies and the Yugoslavs to a serious test. The Allies regarded Yugoslav claims in Austria and elsewhere as excessive. After meeting Bogumil Vošnjak, a Slovene member of the delegation, on 24 January 1919, Harold Nicolson described him as 'very imperialistic'.[3] The Yugoslavs, on the other hand, objected to Article 59 of the draft Austrian Treaty, which concerned the protection of minorities, obliging the Serb-Croat-Slovene state to sign a separate treaty with the Allied and Associated Powers in this respect.

The Yugoslavs pointed out that they were one of the Allies, not a defeated country; Serbia had been a sovereign state, not part of Austria-Hungary. Therefore, Yugoslavia should not be treated the same as, for instance, Hungary. Moreover, a reference in the preamble to Serbia's territorial gains of 1913 raised further objections from the Yugoslav delegation. These territories were inhabited by a non-Serb, Albanian and Macedonian majority. However, Pašić argued, not without reason, that the new territories had been awarded to Serbia by the peace treaties which ended the Balkan Wars. Since that had happened well before the outbreak of the First World War, Pašić pointed out that it was beyond the remit of the Paris Peace Conference to deal with these treaties in any way. The Yugoslav delegation was not the only one that found the article unacceptable – the Romanians objected on similar grounds, also initially refusing to sign the Treaty. Despite heavy pressure from the Americans, the British and the French, the Yugoslavs maintained their point of view. The most they were willing to concede was that somehow the minorities treaty made it clear that only formerly Habsburg territories of the Serb-Croat-Slovene Kingdom were to be bound by it, not Serbia. The Allies, however, would not compromise.

In their view, the annexation of the new territories by Serbia in 1912–13 had not been formally recognised by the Great Powers because the First World War had broken out soon afterwards. Another issue that arose was that the Kingdom of Serbs, Croats and Slovenes was still bound by the terms of the 1878 Congress of Berlin, by virtue of being a legal successor to the Kingdom of Serbia. A special proviso had been inserted in the Treaty, discharging the Serb-Croat-Slovene state from obligations undertaken by Serbia in 1878. But, while the Allies felt that the pre-1912 Serbian state fulfilled its obligations regarding minorities as undertaken at Berlin, post-1913 Serbia had turned into a multi-ethnic state. According to a contemporary account: '[T]he territories acquired [by Serbia] in 1913, which included Macedonia and districts inhabited by Albanians, had a population of so composite a character that here above all some kind of safeguard seemed desirable in the interests of Serbia herself, and certainly for the general pacification of the Balkans. In the Treaty of Constantinople, by which Macedonia had been handed over by Turkey to Serbia, there were clauses securing to the Mussulman population fullest freedom for the continued use of their religion; but on the other hand, nothing was said about the Christians, and unfortunately in the past the feeling between the different Christian races inhabiting Macedonia had been much more bitter than that between the Christians and the Mussulmans.'[4]

The impasse over the Austrian Treaty was related to the signing of the Treaty with Bulgaria, which included a similar provision on the protection of minorities. The Allies threatened to abandon Yugoslav interests in the Adriatic as well as Bulgaria if the delegation did not sign the St Germain document.

With no solution imminent, Pašić, Trumbić, Smodlaka and Ribarž returned temporarily to Belgrade to discuss the crisis with the government. On 20 October they met with Prime Minister Ljuba Davidović and his cabinet (the Democrat Davidović had previously replaced the Radical Protić). Trumbić argued that despite the problematic article on minorities, the Treaty with Austria should be signed. Otherwise, he believed, the continued refusal would surely result in the loss of American support, which was vital for the country's struggle with Italy over the eastern Adriatic. Once again, interests in the Adriatic conflicted with interests elsewhere. And, once again, Croats and Serbs seemingly stood divided. However, Trumbić's arguments swayed Pašić and Davidović. The delegation would sign the Austrian Treaty, but not before making one final attempt to change the Allies' mind regarding Article 59.

Following the delegates' return to Paris, a formal request was submitted to the Allies to exclude the Serbian territory from the Treaty. The reply was again a firm no, and it also carried a threat: either sign both treaties, with Austria and Bulgaria, or none! Just in case the Yugoslavs harboured any hopes the Allies might change their mind, Trumbić was informed by Pichon that this was the final answer. Nevertheless, Pašić sent a formal note to Clemenceau on 5 November, asking again for Serbia's territories to be excluded from the minorities provision. Clemenceau would not budge, so the Yugoslavs gave in at last. This they did on 5 December 1919, when Pašić, Trumbić and Žolger reluctantly added their signatures to the Treaty of St Germain.

The Treaty stipulated that the status of the disputed region of Klagenfurt be settled by a plebiscite. After much negotiation and preparation, the plebiscite was held in October 1920. Disappointingly for the Yugoslavs, a majority voted in favour of staying in Austria, although the result was pretty close. In a remarkably high turnout of nearly 96 per cent, 22,025 voters opted for Austria and 15,279 for Yugoslavia.[5]

Not long before the Yugoslavs finally put their pen to the Treaty of St Germain, they had also signed the treaty with Bulgaria.

The Treaty of Neuilly

The week that preceded the signing of the Bulgarian Treaty was a dramatic one. The Allies informed the delegation that the definite date for the signing of the Treaty had been set for 27 November, and that all outstanding issues had to be resolved 48 hours beforehand. The day before the 'deadline', the delegation decided to sign both the Bulgarian and the Austrian Treaties. Bošković resigned in protest – Davidović accepted his resignation – but remained in Paris to continue his work on reparations issues.

Prime Minister Davidović then suddenly sent instructions to the delegation that it must not sign the financial protocols of the two treaties, since these provided for the whole of Yugoslavia paying the reparation for the former Austro-Hungarian provinces; in effect, that would mean that Serbia, a victim and a victor, would be paying war reparations. Yugoslavia was not the only country facing this seemingly illogical situation: all countries which included former Habsburg territory were also expected to contribute towards reparations, including Italy. By the terms of the St Germain Treaty, Poland, Romania, Yugoslavia and Czechoslovakia were to pay in total 1.5 billion French francs in gold, as their contribution towards Austro-Hungarian reparations.[6]

Trumbić was upset by Davidović's directive, not least because it overruled a previously agreed decision. The Allied verdict that Yugoslavia should contribute towards paying Austria-Hungary's reparations was initially strongly resisted by the Yugoslavs, and the Serbs in particular. The latter understandably hated having to pay towards Austro-Hungarian reparations and felt that Serbia should receive compensation, not contribute towards paying it. Moreover, as Slobodan Jovanović had pointed out at a meeting of the delegation held back in May, if the Yugoslav state accepted the proposition that all former Habsburg territories should contribute to the late Empire's reparation payments, it would *de facto* agree with Italy's argument that Yugoslav territories formerly under Habsburg sovereignty were 'enemy lands'.[7] Nevertheless, due to Allied pressure, Belgrade eventually instructed the delegation to sign the financial protocols as well. Following the government's U-turn, the whole delegation offered to resign. Trumbić proposed that the solution to the problem of reparations might be in taking a public loan, to be spent in Serbia but repaid exclusively by the former Habsburg provinces, so that Serbia would not have to pay any reparations.[8]

Despite the threat of resignation – an act not known to the Allies at the time – the delegation signed the Treaty of Neuilly, including the financial and minorities provisions. In what a British contemporary – clearly not too sympathetic to Bulgaria – described as 'a model of how to draw a just and moderate strategic frontier',[9] Yugoslavia gained some 1,500 square kilometres of territory, including several strategic locations, with a population of around 100,000, mostly ethnic Bulgarians. The Yugoslavs received most, but not all, of the territory they claimed – Vidin and the surrounding areas remained in Bulgaria. In addition, the Treaty imposed strict limitations on Bulgaria's military capability, as demanded not just by the Yugoslavs, but also Greeks and Romanians. It provided for a reduction of Bulgaria's armed forces to 33,000 men, forbade compulsory military service and seriously restricted the country's military industry.[10]

The Treaty of Trianon
By the terms of the Treaty of Trianon, the Serb-Croat-Slovene state received most, if not all, of the territory it

claimed in Bačka, Baranja and western and central parts of the Banat. Yugoslav claims in south Hungary were contested by Hungary and Romania. Hungary, burdened by the stigma of a defeated Central Power, and yet a fragile new country beset by political and social upheavals, could not, as much as it tried, resist the Yugoslav claims. Romania, however, posed a much more formidable opponent. The Treaty was signed a year after a major crisis seriously threatened to undermine the fragile peace in East-Central Europe.

Encouraged by the seemingly imminent Allied intervention against the Bolshevik regime of Béla Kun in Hungary and sensing an opportunity to seize territory it coveted, Romania launched a successful military counter-offensive against the Hungarians in late July 1919, capturing Budapest in early August. The Romanians were not the only regional power asked by the Allies to take part in the military intervention – the Czechoslovaks and the Yugoslavs were also expected to contribute troops. Like the Romanians, the Yugoslavs sensed an opportunity to secure their claims in the north. At the same time, however, Belgrade received an order from the Allied commander General Franchet d'Esperey to withdraw troops from parts of the Banat. Both the government and the delegation protested. Pašić discussed the matter with Clemenceau, and General Pešić with Marshal Foch, and in the end the order was not carried out. In late July, the Yugoslavs put 18,600 soldiers at the Allies' disposal. The intervention in fact never took place, largely because Wilson had been opposed to it from the start. Its very possibility, however, led to further divisions within the delegation, mirroring those among the 'Big Three'. Pašić, like Clemenceau and Lloyd George, was in favour, while Trumbić, sharing Wilson's position, was against. Trumbić believed it would be an *unforgivable mistake if even a single* [*Yugoslav*] *soldier marched on* [*Buda-*]*Pest*. Pašić, on the other hand, spoke of the need to establish democracy in Hungary, but in reality saw a good opportunity to secure desired territories.[11]

In the meantime, intelligence reports reached the Yugoslavs that Bucharest planned to take the opportunity to try to expel Serbian forces from the Banat. The Belgrade government and the delegation sought help from the Allies as well as from Czechoslovakia and Greece. Both Foch and Venizelos promised to send troops to Yugoslavia's aid if Bulgaria were to attack. At the same time, Trumbić approached Edvard Beneš of the Czechoslovak delegation, who promised 'limited' military aid and full diplomatic support in case of a Romanian attack. Beneš explained that the Czechoslovaks were not in a position to intervene militarily on the Yugoslavs' behalf, lest Poland take the opportunity to attack Czechoslovakia; the two countries were involved in a bitter dispute over the Teschen district (Tešin in Czech; Cieszyn in Polish). A regional conflict seemed probable, but was avoided in the end, thanks to firm action by the Allies – the French in particular – who told Brătianu in no uncertain terms that they would not tolerate military intervention in the Banat.[12] By the end of August, Yugoslav troops were firmly in possession of Bačka, Baranja and the parts of the Banat Yugoslavia claimed. Brătianu left Paris in protest and soon resigned as Prime Minister, disappointed with the outcome of the Banat question.

The delegation discharged

Three days before the Treaty of Trianon was signed, Pašić announced he was leaving the delegation. In a telegram to Vesnić (who had become Prime Minister in May that year) he argued he was no longer needed since the delegation had all but completed its mission in Paris. Besides, a consensus existed both within the delegation and between the delegation and the government on all outstanding issues. At a time of financial crisis, Pašić added, it was better to save money by sending him back home, where, in any case, he had important political and private work to continue. The government accepted Pašić's resignation, expressing the hope that he would continue to make himself available should the need for his services arise. It also decided to discharge the delegation, believing that it had done as much as it could and that there was no reason for its continued activity. However, Trumbić and Bošković would remain in Paris in order to work on issues related to reparations. Trumbić attempted to persuade Pašić to change his mind and asked Vesnić to keep the delegation in Paris, since important matters, including the Adriatic question, remained unfinished. All delegates, including Pašić, agreed that it was too early to send the delegation home. Nevertheless, Pašić insisted his decision to resign was final.[13]

At 6.00 p.m. on 30 June, the delegation met at its usual venue at the Hotel Beau-Site. Pašić announced he would be leaving for Belgrade soon. In chair, for the last time, he conveyed a message from Prime Minister Vesnić that he would be unable to attend the Inter-Allied Conferences in Brussels and Spa, and so it was necessary for the delegates to continue their work a little longer; therefore, Vesnić requested that the questions of Pašić's resignation and the discharging of the delegation were to be postponed for the time being. Pašić welcomed the possibility of the delegation continuing its work, but said that it would have to be without him; his resignation was irrevocable. In what was effectively a resignation speech, he said:

All these months we have worked on a very difficult job.

We have not achieved every goal, many issues have not been resolved in our favour, while many remain unsolved, and prospects for us are grim. Nevertheless, we may afford to be satisfied, in the sense that we have always given our best in order to achieve most favourable results. It should be borne in mind that our delegation arrived in Paris to attend the Peace Conference under very difficult circumstances. We faced two odious international treaties concluded by our allies without our participation and without us being consulted, but against us and our interests. These are the London Treaty between Italy and the great Allied powers, and the treaty between these same powers and Romania. Italy and Romania entered the war on the basis of these two treaties, and came to the Peace Conference to demand their implementation. The two treaties, especially the London one, have been the source of our greatest problems at the Peace Conference. Because of the London Treaty we are forced to sacrifice, in the face of Italian demands, a large number of our Slovenian brothers. Internal developments in Italy give me the reason to believe that sooner or later a revolution will break out over there, and present us with an opportunity to gradually achieve the complete liberation and unification of our people, or to at least secure full autonomy for them [Yugoslavs in Italy]. However, summarising our results at this moment, I believe that we have achieved quite a lot.

At the end, I ask my colleagues to forgive me if I have, in moments when my nerves got the better of me, due to tiredness and old age, spoken a harsh word. There occurred at times amongst us differences in opinion, but I am pleased to be able to state that within our Delegation there were no [deep divisions] as in some other Delegations. I am leaving tomorrow, and if you ever remember me and feel the need to hear my opinion or seek advice from an old man, I would be pleased [to oblige]; I remain at your disposal.

Following Bošković's brief praise of Pašić's role at the Conference, Trumbić took the floor. He agreed with Pašić that the delegation had faced an extremely difficult task, stating – clearly incorrectly – that *our state did not have a single true friend at the Peace Conference. Nevertheless, we have had success, but that was mainly the result of the work done by Serbia and its army [during the First World War]. Yet, our Delegation has made a contribution to those successes.* Trumbić then thanked Pašić for his *brotherly patience. There were differences in opinion among us, but never a conflict*, Trumbić said. At the end, he asked Pašić, in the name of all the delegates, to reconsider his resignation.

Pašić thanked Trumbić, but would not reconsider. All he would promise was that he might return one day, in a personal capacity and only if needed and if his health and circumstances allowed him.

Finally, Ribarž expressed his gratitude to Pašić, for himself and in the name of all Slovenes, 'our smallest tribe that has caused the Delegation the greatest problems'. 'But', he hastened to add, 'it should not be forgotten that the Slovenian tribe has given the greatest sacrifice at this time', clearly referring to the failure of the delegation to secure more territory in Austria and Trieste. Nevertheless, 'Mr Pašić's contribution in the defence of the Slovene part of our people is well known to all Slovenes and they will remain forever grateful to him', the Slovene delegate concluded.

These turned out to be the last words spoken at a meeting of the Political Section. Two days later, a cable from the government confirmed that the Kingdom of Serbs, Croats and Slovenes was to withdraw its delegates from Paris, considering their mission over. It fell to Trumbić to officially inform delegates of the news. By 15 July the delegation had been discharged. Apart from Pašić, Trumbić and Ribarž, also present at the final meeting were Bošković, Radović of the Montenegrin Section, and Colonel Danilo Kalafatović of the Military Section. The meeting, and the mission of the delegation of the Kingdom of Serbs, Croats and Slovenes, ended at 8.20 p.m., 30 June 1920, a year and a half after the delegation of the 'Kingdom of Serbia' had convened in Paris.[14]

Nikola Pašić

III
The Legacy

10
Aftermath and Epilogue

The peace delegation of the Kingdom of Serbs, Croats and
Slovenes began to assemble in Paris in early January 1919
without much preparation but with many uncertainties surrounding it. The country had been proclaimed the previous
month amid chaos, insecurity and euphoria, following four
years of the hitherto most destructive war in human history.
The Yugoslavs had formed Yugoslavia on the premise of the
national self-determination of the three-named nation of
Serbs, Croats and Slovenes, but an enormous task of unifying
different traditions, cultures and legal and economic systems
awaited them. The building had to be carried out simultaneously with the rebuilding both of destroyed infrastructure
and of societies deeply scarred by war.

Pašić and Trumbić, the leaders of the delegation, did not
get on, their differences originating in conflicting wartime
visions of a future Yugoslav state. Yugoslavia's allies did not
recognise the country's delegation in Paris. Its major opponent was Italy, one of the powers running the Peace Conference. Yet, the delegation also enjoyed some advantages:
Serbia's prestige was high due to its heroic contribution to

Europe 1923

FINLAND

Petrograd (St Petersburg)

Tallinn
ESTONIA

Riga
LATVIA

Sea

LITHUANIA

anzig

Vilnius

Königsberg
EAST
PRUSSIA

Warsaw

Brest-Litovsk

POLAND

Moscow

**UNION OF SOVIET
SOCIALIST REPUBLICS**

Kiev

VAKIA

Budapest

GARY

ROMANIA

Odessa

Belgrade

Bucharest

OSLAVIA

BULGARIA
Sofia

Black Sea

na
BANIA

Istanbul

GREECE

Athens

TURKEY

IRAQ

SYRIA

CYPRUS

the war effort, and their internal differences notwithstanding, Pašić and Trumbić shared a common goal – international recognition of the Serb-Croat-Slovene Kingdom in as extended borders as possible – and were determined to fulfil it. Both men were experienced politicians, supported, in most cases, by highly competent colleagues, the Yugoslav claims largely – but not entirely – concerned territories populated by South Slavs, and the new Serb-Croat-Slovene army was in control of much of the Yugoslav territory. In the sympathetic President Wilson, and in the principle of national self-determination, they had two powerful weapons with which to counter the rival claims of their neighbours. By the time the delegation left Paris in July 1920, it had secured international recognition of the country and most of the territories it had originally claimed. The exception was the dispute with Italy over the eastern Adriatic, which could not be settled in Paris. It would eventually be resolved in Rapallo in November 1920, to the full satisfaction of neither side. The Yugoslavs made major concessions, but so did the Italians. The new state appeared politically and economically viable and its future seemed bright. As did that of the new international order created in Paris, of which Yugoslavia would be a 'worthy member', as Vesnić optimistically proclaimed in January 1920.

Like most of Europe, Yugoslavia would remain unstable throughout the inter-war period. The international predicament, partly dealt with in this book, was relatively benign when compared with problems at home. Unrest in Kosovo and Macedonia and alienation among many Montenegrins and Croats because of the way Yugoslavia had been united, not to mention the socio-economic consequences of the war, would have posed a major challenge to states far longer established than the newly formed Serb-Croat-Slovene Kingdom.

Yet, by the early to mid-1920s the country seemed to have overcome most of its initial problems, some of which had temporarily threatened its existence.

It was the Serb-Croat question that was central to the country's (in)stability during the inter-war years. The relationship between Pašić and Trumbić was symptomatic of the wider Serb-Croat dynamics in Yugoslavia. Pašić's views were Serbo-centric, meaning that Yugoslavia was to be based on the successful Serbian model of a centralised nation-state. Trumbić's Croatian perspective preferred a decentralised state, possibly on a dual Serb-Croat basis. But, in 1919 dual and 'complex' states represented a defeated model, whereas 'simple' nation states appeared to be the future.

The reasons for the disagreements within the delegation and between Pašić and Trumbić should not be sought in some old Serb-Croat animosity. In addition to their mutually competing visions of a united Yugoslavia and of a clash of two strong personalities, differences emerged partly due to another conflict of ideologies: the nationality principle vs *Realpolitik*. The contest between Wilsonian principles and traditional diplomacy was of course symptomatic of the whole Conference.

Trumbić understandably believed that insisting on national self-determination placed the Yugoslavs in Dalmatia and the north-west Adriatic in a superior position over Italy. Of all the Yugoslav claims, those in the eastern Adriatic were the strongest because they rested on the nationality principle. Yet, they were also the most vulnerable because of Italy's competing claims. Demands elsewhere were not so clearly supported by the nationality principle, but had much more chance of success because they competed with the aspirations of defeated countries, with the important exception of Romania. Serbia's – and Pašić's – old allies, Britain and France, encouraged the Yugoslavs to sacrifice territory in the eastern Adriatic in exchange for 'compensation' in the north and east and possibly south. Wilson, on the other hand, openly sided with the Yugoslavs in their contest with the Italians. These mixed messages from the principal Allies contributed to divisions among the Yugoslavs.

> Between us, the Serbs and the Croats, there are no differences. It has been our [Serbs'] centuries-long desire to liberate ourselves and unite with our brothers.
>
> PAŠIĆ TO CLEMENCEAU, JANUARY 1919[1]

Pašić's thinking in Paris was influenced by several factors. First, he behaved as the leader of a victorious power that should be rewarded for its victory with additional territory of strategic importance, especially for Belgrade and Serbia. Secondly, as a native of eastern Serbia, his views were shaped by Serb-Bulgarian rivalry, not just over Macedonia, and the recent experience of brutal Bulgarian occupation of parts of Serbia. He was determined that Bulgaria should be punished and weakened to the extent that it would never be in a position to invade Serbia again. Pašić's views were still very much those of a Serbian leader, not of a representative of the newly-formed Yugoslav state.

In any case compromises between the principle of nationality and the old diplomacy had to be made and were made: among the Yugoslavs and among the Allies. Trumbić and Pašić were rivals, but they were also allies who, despite all their differences, achieved considerable success in Paris, as they had during the course of the war.

As for the post-war order, Pašić did not share Trumbić's idealism in respect of international peace – or Wilson's, for that matter. In that respect, his views were comparable to those of another veteran European statesmen – Clemenceau. A direct participant in various wars between 1875 and 1918, Pašić believed in 1919 that the Great Powers were merely recuperating before another inevitable confrontation. Unfortunately, events would prove him right, though it is debatable whether even he could have foreseen the extent of violence and destruction that would erupt only twenty years later in a global conflict that was fought between the opponents and the defenders of the Paris settlement.

Pašić and Trumbić after the Conference

In 1919 it looked as if the Peace Conference would mark the end of a distinguished political career, due to Pašić's advanced age and a damaged relationship with Prince Regent Alexander, whose influence in the political life of the country was considerable. At the same time, it seemed as if Trumbić – twenty years younger and with better 'Yugoslav credentials' – was destined to become the political leader of the new country. However, it would turn out that Pašić had another political life after Paris, while Trumbić's career at the top end of politics virtually ended soon afterwards. Paris was to be Trumbić's zenith, but for Pašić it represented a short break before a return to dominating the politics of his country one final time.

It is hard to determine to what extent the paths the careers of Pašić and Trumbić took after Paris were due to their own actions and to what degree these were symptomatic of the way Yugoslavia's political life developed. It is probably the case that both factors played a part. In retrospect, it is regrettable that Trumbić did not emerge as one of Yugoslavia's principal political leaders after the Conference. Ten years later, King Alexander allegedly thought so. 'Why didn't he [Trumbić] listen to me when I advised him after Rapallo that he should not join any political party?', Alexander asked the sculptor Ivan Meštrović, a former member of the Yugoslav Committee who was on friendly terms with both the King and Trumbić, in August 1930. 'This era would have been ideal for him. Yugoslavism for which we fought in the war could not be implemented immediately, there were obstacles. Now is the time. If he had listened to me, he would now be one of the leading [political figures].' Alexander was wrong: Trumbić did not join any political party after Rapallo, but initially pursued a political career as an independent MP, before forming his own political party in the mid-1920s. In any case, a Croatian journalist close to the King later told Trumbić that Alexander was 'yearning' to re-establish 'direct and personal contacts' with him.[2] It is, of course, debatable whether Trumbić would have cooperated with a dictatorship, and in any event he had long abandoned his earlier Yugo-slavism by the time the conversation between Alexander and Meštrović took place.

Following the signing of the Rapallo Treaty, Trumbić returned home. With the Adriatic question off the agenda, he resigned as Foreign Minister in December that year, keeping his word. In late November he had been elected to the Con-stituent Assembly as an independent candidate. There, he would once again square up to his old opponent Pašić, whose Radical Party was pushing for a centralist Constitu-tion. Trumbić complained to Slobodan Jovanović that he had lost all contact with Pašić and the Prince Regent. He asked Jovanović to convey his message to them: it would be a grave mistake to impose the centralism of old Serbia on the Croats, who should be offered some form of autonomy, however minimal. A centralist Constitution would impede any possi-bility of a Serb-Croat agreement, he warned. *If I were certain that Serbs understood the dangers of centralism, I would go to Zagreb tomorrow to start a [political] struggle against [Stjepan] Radić*, Trumbić told Jovanović.[3]

Trumbić was not the only opponent of Pašić's centralism. Smodlaka and Korošec offered alternative constitutional proposals, as did Protić. They all argued in favour of a decentralised state – a compromise between centralism and federalism. But Pašić, supported by Davidović and the main Muslim parties, and in the absence of Stjepan Radić's Peasants, the new dominant political force in Croatia, was able to have his way. The first, highly centralist, Constitution of the Kingdom of Serbs, Croats and Slovenes was promulgated on 28 June 1921.

The triumph in the constitutional battle symbolised Pašić's return to the very top of his country's political pyramid and the beginning of his domination of Yugoslav politics in the first half of the 1920s. Yet, his victory would prove to be pyrrhic in the long run. Instead of bringing stability, the Constitution destabilised the country's political life throughout a decade which began with such promise, but ended in tragedy. One of Pašić's greatest political errors was that he misunderstood, and possibly underestimated, Croat opposition to centralism. He mistakenly treated the Croatian Peasant Party like any other political party, when in reality it was a national movement. Even Pašić did not command as much support among the Serbs as did Radić among the Croats in the 1920s. The Croatian Peasant Party regularly received around 90 per cent of the Croat vote during the inter-war period, which no Serb-dominated party could achieve. Pašić erroneously believed that the Croat question could be solved by merely including Croat parties in government.[4]

Pašić served as Prime Minister of the Serb-Croat-Slovene Kingdom for the entire period between January 1921 and

April 1926, with the exception of Davidović's '100-day' government in 1924. He headed ten different cabinets – a sign of political instability that was neither unique to Yugoslavia nor to East-Central Europe in general. The average six-month Pašić cabinet was not much different from the average lifespan of a cabinet in the French Third and Fourth Republics.[5] Yet, such frequent elections and cabinet reshuffles suggest that even the largest political party in Yugoslavia was not strong enough to form stable, long-lasting governments. Pašić was able to stay in government so long largely because he always found a willing coalition partner: the Slovenes, the Bosnian Muslims, Pribićević's Independent Democrats ... and in 1925, even Radić's Croat Peasants. The first half of the 1920s marked the final phase of an extremely successful career in politics which took off properly with Pašić's election to the Serbian parliament in 1878.

There was life after Paris for Pašić's Balkan counterparts, too: Brătianu, having resigned in 1919, returned to office in Romania three years later and served as Prime Minister for another four years; as did Venizelos in late 1920s and early 1930s Greece. The exception was the unfortunate Stamboliĭski, murdered in Bulgaria in 1923. For the 'Big Four', on the other hand, Paris represented the zenith of their careers, with Lloyd George, who remained in office the longest, falling from power by 1922.

Although Trumbić was only 56 when the Peace Conference ended, and even though he appeared a natural leader of a united Yugoslavia, he would never again reach the same political heights and would play a relatively insignificant role during the inter-war period. There were three main reasons for this: firstly, Pašić's concept of a Serb-dominated, centralist Yugoslavia prevailed during the formative period of the South Slav state. Secondly, the period saw the emergence, with the introduction of universal male suffrage in the former Habsburg territories, of Stjepan Radić's Croatian Peasant Party. Radić's political programme was based more on the national question than on peasant politics, and, as already noted, he would receive the vast majority of Croat votes during the 1920s. Trumbić, a believer in a unitary Serb-Croat-Slovene nation, but an opponent of centralism, was never likely to attract a majority support in Yugoslavia at the time. Pašić's Serb-style Yugoslav centralism and Radić's Croat-centric populism were much more successful in attracting voters in a society as polarised as that of the Kingdom of Serbs, Croats and Slovenes. It was one of Trumbić's major disappointments that Davidović's Democrats had sided with Pašić in the debate over the Constitution. Trumbić and the former Independent Radicals, who had provided the core for the Democratic Party, more often than not had stood together in opposition to Pašić during the war and Trumbić had hoped they would be natural post-war allies. Thirdly, Trumbić may have been an exceptionally gifted lawyer and campaigner – RW Seton-Watson described him as 'the most brilliant advocate' whose 'powers of argument, though perhaps somewhat prolix according to Western standards, reached memorable heights'[6] – but he was ultimately not a great politician. Pašić frequently outmanoeuvred him, while Radić probably used him for his contacts in Belgrade and influence among pro-Yugoslav Croats. Trumbić was perhaps too egotistical and individual to truly succeed in politics.[7]

> There are no ethnic differences between the Serbs and the Croats, but there are differences in mentality that stem from the past.
> **TRUMBIĆ, APRIL 1921[8]**

Gradually, by the mid-1920s, Trumbić had come to abandon unitarism and moved closer to Radić, but only temporarily. In 1925, Pašić and Radić reached an agreement after which the Croatian Peasant Party entered government, with Radić as Education Minister. Trumbić felt betrayed by Radić's U-turn, and in early 1926 he formed the Croatian Federalist Peasant Party, hoping to attract Radić's dissidents. But neither they nor the declining numbers of unitarist Yugoslavs among Croats would join the party *en masse*, and in any case, there were too few of them to challenge Radić seriously. Although Trumbić would be re-elected to parliament in the 1927 elections – the last ever democratic Yugoslav general elections – the Croat Federalists remained a marginal party and would eventually wither away. As for the Radicals, they would enter a period of crisis and long decline following Pašić's death in late 1926, splitting into various factions even before the introduction of King Alexander's 'anti-party' dictatorship in January 1929. Their collaboration with the Croat Peasants proved short-lived, lasting less than two years.

King Alexander introduced dictatorship following the culmination of the political crisis in the summer of 1928. On 20 June, a Radical Party deputy shot five Croat Peasant Party deputies during a particularly heated parliamentary debate, killing two of them. Among those wounded was Radić (whose nephew was one of those killed). The Croat leader initially appeared to have recovered from the operation to remove the assassin's bullets, but died on 8 August. The Croatian Peasants and their allies, predominantly Croatian Serb Independent Democrats led by Pribićević, refused to return to the Belgrade parliament and demanded federalisation of the country. The veteran Slovene leader Korošec briefly headed the government – Trumbić publicly condemned him for accepting the mandate *to spite the Croats*[9] – before King Alexander dissolved parliament, banned political parties and abolished the 1921 Constitution on 6 January 1929, the Old Style or Serbian Orthodox Christmas Eve. Vladko Maček, Radić's successor, welcomed the abolition of the hated Constitution and expressed the hope that the King would solve the Croat question. Even Trumbić allegedly believed that the dictatorship was *perhaps the only way out of the crisis*, providing the King was up to the task.[10]

Trumbić joined the Croatian Peasant Party in 1928, largely as an act of solidarity after the June tragedy. At this time a Frankist deputy called Ante Pavelić also briefly joined the party. When Trumbić visited Radić in hospital, he told the wounded Croat leader that it was time for an even more radical opposition to the regime.[11] Yet he never went as far as Pavelić, who left the country soon afterwards to establish his extremist, separatist *Ustaša* organisation in Italy. Disillusioned and embittered with political developments in the country he helped create, and never really comfortable with the populism of the Croatian Peasants, Trumbić was something of a 'detached' party member and one of Maček's chief political advisors. In late 1928, Trumbić travelled to Vienna, Paris and London to gain support for the Croat cause, but had little success.

Trumbić's activities during this period and some of his statements were anti-Yugoslav, and are sometimes interpreted as separatist. When Dragoljub Jovanović, a Serbian opposition leader, went to Zagreb in the mid-1930s to discuss co-operation between Croat and Serb opposition before forthcoming general elections, he found an angry and radicalised Trumbić. *What elections?! This country needs a revolution, not elections!*, he allegedly told his Serbian visitor. When Jovanović reminded him of his committed Yugoslavism during the war and the Peace Conference – he had heard Trumbić's public lectures as a student in Paris – Trumbić claimed that it was then necessary for Croats to join Serbs, who were one of the Allies, before adding: *It could have all turned out well if your politicians had not ruined everything … I am not abandoning Yugoslavism, but in Belgrade …* He did not finish the sentence, but he was clearly suggesting that the regime was pushing him away from his support for Yugoslavia.[12]

Throughout his life, Trumbić was concerned with the Croat question. By the early 20th century he had come to believe that it could be solved only in a Yugoslav state, together with Serbia and the Serbs (not unlike Pašić's realisation that pan-Serb unification could only be achieved in Yugoslavia, together with Croats and Slovenes). But by the late 1920s, Trumbić no longer saw Yugoslavia as the only framework for the solution of the Croat question. The Yugoslav framework was in his view increasingly unacceptable; not because he did not want it to be, but because the reality was telling him otherwise. Yet, he was not a separatist, certainly not in the mould of Pavelić.[13] If during any period of his career he could be described as a separatist, it was during his activities against Austria-Hungary, especially once the war broke out.

In November 1932 Trumbić was one of the main authors of an opposition manifesto known as the 'Zagreb Points', issued by leading Croat and Croatian Serb politicians. The manifesto blamed centralism for the country's political crisis. The only way out of the crisis was to renegotiate the terms of the union, and replace the centralist arrangement with a dualist/federal one. The 'Zagreb Points' triggered a sequence of similar opposition resolutions in Ljubljana, Sarajevo and Belgrade, and led to Maček's arrest. Maček would be released from prison only after King Alexander's assassination in October 1934 – in the meantime, Trumbić was *de facto* one of the party leaders. King Alexander's assassination in Marseilles, while on a state visit to France, was a joint Macedonian Revolutionary-*Ustaša* operation; the French Foreign Minister Louis Barthou was also killed. A pro-Maček journal published a touching obituary of the monarch, of which Trumbić was allegedly one of the authors.[14]

The Croat-Serb co-operation in opposition gathered momentum in the second half of the 1930s, with Maček, Davidović and Pribićević and his successors (the leader of the Serbs in Croatia had died in 1936) seriously challenging governments formed by Pašić's successors, Korošec's Slovene Populists and Bosnian Muslims. Ironically, Trumbić, who played such a crucial role during the unification of Yugoslavia and at the Paris Peace Conference, opposed the co-operation with Belgrade, even with the Serbian democratic opposition. Eventually, in August 1939 Maček reached an agreement with Prince Regent Paul and Prime Minister Dragiša Cvetković, an unremarkable younger follower of Pašić. Croatia was given self-rule, and Maček was appointed Deputy Prime Minister of Yugoslavia. Along with Trumbić, he was the highest-ranking Croat in inter-war Yugoslav governments.

Trumbić did not live long enough to see the establishment of an autonomous Croatia within Yugoslavia. He had died the previous November, in his native Split, aged 74. His death was commemorated by three different sides: the Croatian Peasant Party, the anti-Yugoslav Frankists (close, but not necessarily identical to the *Ustašas*), and the government. The Croatian Peasants celebrated his life as an ally of Radić and Maček and as a Croat patriot, as did the Frankists, though they emphasised his early career as a member of Starčević's Party of Rights.

The official commemoration emphasised his Yugoslavism and praised his role in the creation of Yugoslavia. All three sides had a point – Trumbić had been all these things at different stages of his illustrious, but ultimately unfulfilled career.

Trumbić's most important legacy was his role in the creation of Yugoslavia. Pašić, on the other hand, left a deeper and more complex legacy, as one of the founders of Yugoslavia, but also as one of the greatest Serb leaders of modern times. Pašić's legacy is controversial – non-Serbs tend to accuse him of establishing Serb control in the Serb-Croat-Slovene state and contributing to the country's instability, while some Serbs blame him for choosing Yugoslavia instead of a Greater Serbia (even if, in reality, there was no choice). Trumbić's legacy is not uncontroversial, either: he helped create a state many Croats came to resent. This may be the reason why today even in Croatia Trumbić remains a relatively obscure historical figure, while Pašić is well known across former Yugoslavia.

Only 19 months after the 1939 Croat-Serb agreement, inter-war Yugoslavia was invaded and dismembered by Nazi Germany, Fascist Italy and their allies. The Cvetković-Maček government signed the Tripartite Pact on 25 March 1941, but was overthrown by a military *coup* two days later. The Yugoslav public, mostly Serb and Slovene, enthusiastically supported the rejection of the Pact. However, on 6 April the country was attacked by the Axis Powers, and eleven days later it was defeated and partitioned. An enlarged Croatia, including Bosnia-Herzegovina and most of Vojvodina, but without the majority of Dalmatia, which Italy took at last, was proclaimed independent under Pavelić's Nazi-puppet regime. A significantly reduced Serbia, with the Banat, was placed under German military occupation, with a collaborationist administration installed later in the year (although its jurisdiction did not extend to the Banat, where many ethnic Germans lived). Just over twenty years after Pašić and Trumbić had secured Yugoslavia's borders and helped the country gain international recognition at Versailles, the South Slav union, like the Versailles order, was in its death throes. It was symbolic that the Yugoslav capitulation was signed on 17 April by General Kalafatović; who, then a colonel, was a member of the Serb-Croat-Slovene delegation in Paris and attended the very last meeting of the political delegation.

'Versailles Yugoslavia'?

That Yugoslavia is still sometimes labelled a 'Versailles creation' has less to do with poor history than with daily politics. Ever since its emergence, those opposing Yugoslavia have labelled it an unnatural creation of an artificial settlement created in Paris in 1919–20. Opponents of inter-war Yugoslavia were also enemies of Versailles. Even though the country was obviously not created by the Great Powers at the Peace Conference, it may be worth comparing briefly the 'Versailles order' and the 'South Slav settlement' at the end of the First World War, which resulted in the united Kingdom of Serbs, Croats and Slovenes.

A historian of the Versailles Treaty (who also happened to be one of the leading historians of Yugoslavia) wrote in relation to the Treaty: '[T]he Versailles Settlement comprised elements of morality and idealism, unique in the history of peacemaking, with old-fashioned power politics. It changed the political map of Europe. In so doing, "Versailles" inevitably had its beneficiaries as well as its victims. The former saw it as the fulfilment of national self-determination; the latter as a grievous *Diktat*. Much has been said for either case. Yet the statesmen of 1919 acted in the belief that they were the first to be governed by principles that would result in fairness for all and an enduring, stable peace.'[15]

The same could be said of Yugoslavia. Its creation required elements of both morality and idealism, of political pragmatism and *Realpolitik* and genuine belief that Yugoslavs were members of a single nation who should be united in their own state. If the Paris Peace Conference had its beneficiaries and its losers, so too did the Yugoslav settlement. The clear victors at the time were the South Slavs, not only the Serbs as is usually assumed, while the main losers were those large ethnic minorities that found themselves in a new and in many respects alien country; ethnic Albanians, Hungarians, Germans and Italians, as well as Macedonian Slavs, whom no one recognised as such at the time. The Yugoslavs saw Yugoslavia as the fulfillment of their long struggle for national liberation and unification, while the non-Yugoslavs saw the South Slav state as an imposition by the victors of the First World War. Just like the peacemakers, the makers of Yugoslavia acted in a belief that they would produce a just and long-lasting settlement.

Losers at Paris continued to seek change of the borders and the terms imposed by the settlement. Yet, it was not always easy to distinguish losers from victors. Italy was nominally a victor, but felt dissatisfied with the settlement. Yugoslavs who had lived in formerly Habsburg territories were nominally losers, but found themselves on a victorious side thanks to their alliance with Serbia and the creation of the Yugoslav state. Yet, within a decade following Versailles, many of them, arguably, would feel as alienated from Belgrade as they did from Budapest and Vienna. In the second half of the 1930s, many Serbs, too, would begin to question their wisdom in 'creating' Yugoslavia.

Following the Axis destruction of the country in 1941, a complex set of ideological, ethnic, liberation and collaborationist wars broke out on the territory of the first former Yugoslavia. By 1945, approximately a million people had died, half of them Serbs; among the South Slavs, proportionally Montenegrins and Bosnian Muslims suffered even heavier casualties, and Croats suffered almost as much.[16] Yet, a Yugoslavia re-emerged, this time as a communist-governed federation. Ironically, the Communists, once among those calling for the break-up of 'Versailles Yugoslavia' as an artificial, bourgeois creation, were now arguably the only group capable of organising an effective, multi-ethnic resistance and re-establishing a South Slav union.

To quote the historian of the Versailles Treaty again: 'Was it [the Versailles Treaty] just, politically sound, economically capable of fulfilment? Was it indeed the harbinger of a new era of international morality and European stability which many of its advocates so ardently sought? Or were its provisions unduly harsh? Did it in fact sow the seeds of destruction which germinated crisis after crisis and eventually pushed Europe into the abyss of a new war? Was its breakdown caused by the passivity of the victor or by the dynamic resistance of the vanquished? Ultimately, was it foredoomed to failure?'[17]

These same questions apply to Yugoslavia, and have been raised by scholars and non-scholars alike, especially since the Yugoslav Federation broke up violently in the early 1990s, at the end of another international order established after a World War. Attempting to answer them would require another book. What this book has hopefully shown is that the founders of Yugoslavia, despite all their differences, problems and deficiencies, believed that their struggle was just, and that the new country was to be a worthy member of a new international community, based on justice and democracy. Was Yugoslavia an artificial state, doomed to failure from the start? It was artificial in the sense that all states are, to varying degrees. Yugoslavia's creation in 1918 was supported by the South Slav political elites and there was at least some popular enthusiasm among 'ordinary' people. The Allies thought it was a logical project and looked at it with sympathy, even though they did not recognise the new state straight away. Yugoslavia was not their creation, but its external stability depended on the stability of the international order created in Paris in 1919–20. The ultimate failure of the Yugoslav project does not mean that it was doomed from the very start. Yugoslavia was formed and existed in arguably the most violent of centuries. That it survived most of it, suggests it was a worthwhile project. And, who knows, it may yet return one day in another guise within the EU framework. Pašić and Trumbić's work in Paris would in that case probably appear longer-lasting than it seems at present.

Notes

Prelude

1. 'Slovenia' is used for the sake of convenience, even though there was then no territory officially called 'Slovenia'; the Slovenes lived in the historic Austrian provinces of Carinthia, Carniola and Styria. Croatia refers to the historic triune kingdom of Croatia-Slavonia and Dalmatia.

2. *Zapisnici sa sednica delegacije Kraljevine S[rba], H[rvata i] S[lovenaca] na Mirovnoj konferenciji u Parizu 1919–1920*, compiled and edited by Bogdan Krizman and Bogumil Hrabak (Belgrade: [Kultura], 1960) pp 19–20, hereafter *Zapisnici*.

3. *Zapisnici*, pp 23–4.

4. For an elaboration of this argument, see Dejan Djokić, *Elusive Compromise: A History of Interwar Yugoslavia* (London: C Hurst & Co. and New York, Columbia University Press, 2007).

1 Who Were the Yugoslavs?

1. Josip Smodlaka, *Jugoslav Territorial Claims (Lecture delivered by J. Smodlaka, Deputy for Spalato and*

Member of the Peace Conference Delegation of the Kingdom of Serbs, Croats and Slovenes, at a meeting of the Union des Grandes Associations françaises contre la Propagande ennemie, on Tuesday, March 11th 1919) (Paris: 1919) p 4.

2. *Zapisnici*, p 29.

2 Pašić's Serbia

1. See Stevan K Pavlowitch, *Serbia: The History Behind the Name* (London: C Hurst & Co., 2002), Chapters 2–4, for a recent scholarly treatment of Serbia in the 19th century.

2. There is no agreement on the exact date of Pašić's birth, but most sources agree he was born in December 1845.

3. Slobodan Jovanović, 'Nikola Pašić' in *Moji savremenici* (Windsor, CA: Avala, 1962) pp 135–220, is an excellent and insightful analysis written by a contemporary and a member of the Yugoslav delegation in Paris; hereafter Jovanović, 'Pašić'.

4. Jovanović, 'Pašić', p 148. For Pašić's height and 'anthropological' description, see Niko Župani, 'Antropološki ocrt Nikole P. Pašića i Milenka R Vesnića', *Etnolog: Glasnik Kr[aljevskega] Etnografskega Muzeja v Ljubljani*, Vol I (Ljubljana: 1926–7) pp 74–83.

5. Djordje Dj Stanković, *Nikola Pašić i Jugoslovensko pitanje* (Belgrade: BIGZ, 1985) Vol I, p 75, hereafter Stanković, *Pašić i Jugoslovensko pitanje*.

6. Djordje Dj Stanković, *Nikola Pašić, Saveznici i stvaranje Jugoslavije* (Belgrade: BIGZ, 1984) p 21, hereafter Stanković, *Pašić, Saveznici*; Nikola Pašić, *Sloga Srbo-Hrvata* (Belgrade: 1995).

7. Stanković, *Pašić, Saveznici*, p 21; Stanković, *Pašić i Jugoslovensko pitanje*, p 77.
8. Stanković, *Pašić, Saveznici*, p 26.

3 Trumbić and Croatia

1. See Mirjana Gross, 'The Integration of the Croatian Nation', *East European Quarterly*, Vol 15, No 2 (1981) pp 209–25. For a recent scholarly account of Croatia's 19th century, see Ivo Goldstein, *Croatia: A History* (London: C Hurst & Co., 1999) Chapter 6.
2. Ivo Perić, *Ante Trumbić na dalmatinskom političkom poprištu* (Split: Muzej grada Splita, 1984) p 145n, hereafter Perić, *Trumbić*.
3. For details of Trumbić's early life and career see Perić, *Trumbić*, Chapters 1–4. See also Ivo Petrinović's Introduction in Ante Trumbić, *Izabrani politički spisi*. Compiled and introduced by Ivo Petrinović (Zagreb: Golden Marketing: Narodene novine, 1998), hereafter Trumbić, *Izabrani politički spisi*.
4. Perić, *Trumbić*, p 22.
5. Ante Smith Pavelić, *Dr Ante Trumbić: Problemi hrvatsko-srpskih odnosa* (Munich: 1959) p 15.
6. Perić, *Trumbić*, p 100.

4 War and Unification

1. Milorad Ekmečić, *Ratni ciljevi Srbije 1914*, 2nd edn (Belgrade: Politika, 1992) p 89.
2. 'Izjava kr.[aljevske] vlade u Narodnoj Skupštini', Niš, 7 December (24 November OS) 1914, *Dokumenti o postanku Kraljevine Srba, Hrvata i Slovenaca, 1914–1919*, compiled by Ferdo Šišić (Zagreb: 1920) p 10, hereafter Šišić, *Dokumenti*. The coalition government

was formed by Pašić's Radicals, the Independent
Radicals and the Progressives.

3. 'Tekst Londonskoga pakta', in *Jadransko pitanje na
   Konferenciji mira u Parizu. Zbirka akata i dokumenata*,
   complied by Ferdo Šišić (Zagreb: 1920) pp 6–9, p 7.
   The text of the London Treaty was translated from
   *Les Documents secrets des archives du ministère des
   affaires étrangères de Russie, publiés par les Bolcheviks*,
   compiled by Émile Laloy (Paris: 1920). An English
   translation is available in HWV Temperley (ed), *A
   History of the Peace Conference of Paris*, 6 Vols
   (London: Frowde and Hodder & Stoughton, 1920) Vol
   5, pp 384–92, hereafter Temperley, *History*.

4. Cited in Ivo J Lederer, *Yugoslavia at the Paris Peace
   Conference: A Study in Frontiermaking* (New Haven
   and London: Yale University Press, 1963) p 93, hereafter
   Lederer, *Yugoslavia*.

5. Cited in Lederer, *Yugoslavia*, p 12.

6. Lederer, *Yugoslavia*, p 12.

7. Cited in Lederer, *Yugoslavia*, pp 13–14.

8. Dragovan Šepić, *Italija, Saveznici i jugoslavensko
   pitanje, 1914–1918* (Zagreb: Školska Knjiga, 1970)
   pp 138–41.

9. For an interesting brief discussion about Pašić's views
   on Greater Serbia and Yugoslavia, see Jovanović, 'Pašić i
   Jugoslavija', in *Moji savremenici*, pp 218–20.

10. The same hotel where Alexander's grandson and
    namesake would be born in July 1945. An apartment in
    the hotel was proclaimed by the British government to
    be Yugoslav territory for 24 hours, so that the heir to the
    throne could be born in 'Yugoslavia'. At the end of the
    Second World War, the Yugoslav Communist authorities

ousted the Karadjordjević dynasty and banned it from returning to the country.

11. 'Deputation to the Prince Regent: A Nation's Ideal', *The Times,* 6 April 1916.

12. Andrej Mitrović, *Serbia's Great War, 1914–1918* (London: Hurst & Co., 2007) Chapter 6, hereafter Mitrović, *Great War.*

13. For more about this important episode and Pašić's role in it, see David McKenzie, *The 'Black Hand' on Trial: Salonica, 1917* (Boulder: East European Monographs, New York: Distributed by Columbia University Press, 1995).

14. A full text of the Corfu Declaration in English is reproduced in Temperley, *History,* Vol 5, pp 393–6.

15. Ivo Banac, *The National Question in Yugoslavia: Origins, History, Politics* (Ithaca, NY: Cornell University Press, 1994) p 124, hereafter Banac, *The National Question.*

16. Dragoslav Janković, *Jugoslovensko pitanje i Krfska deklaracija 1917. godine* (Belgrade: 1967) p 236.

17. Cited in Hugh and Christopher Seton-Watson, *The Making of a New Europe: R.W. Seton-Watson and the Last Years of Austria-Hungary* (London: Methuen, 1981) p 300. Both Serbian and Yugoslav nationalists viewed Serbia as their equivalent of Piedmont, an Italian kingdom which played a key role in the process of Italian unification in the second half of the 19th century.

18. The 29 October proclamation: Temperley, *History,* Vol 4, p 196; national anthems: Pavlowitch, *Serbia,* p 105; Ljubljana: Janko Pleterski, *Prva odločitev Slovenecev za Jugoslavijo* (Ljubljana: Slovenska matica, 1971) pp 264–5.

19. 'Delegati Narod.[nog] Vijeća pred Regentom Aleksandrom', in Šišić, *Dokumenti*, pp 280–3, p 282.

5 *Délégation du Royaume des Serbes, Croates et Slovènes*

1. Josip Smodlaka, *Zapisi Dra Josipa Smodlake* (Zagreb: 1972) pp 78–87, 90–2, hereafter Smodlaka, *Zapisi*.
2. Quoted in Alan Sharp, *The Versailles Settlement: Peacemaking After the First World War, 1919–1923* 2nd edn (Basingstoke: Palgrave Macmillan, 2008) p 233n, hereafter Sharp, *Versailles*.
3. *Zapisnici*, pp 23–4.
4. *Zapisnici*, p 59. The Croats probably feared that because the name of the state was so long, the country would be called 'Serbia' by the outside world. This is what Ante Tresić-Pavičić told Stevan K Pavlović during a long walk on the streets of Paris in late December 1918, before adding that, even though he was a Croat, he would not mind if that were to happen. Tresić-Pavičić was a member of the Serb-Croat-Slovene peace delegation, while Pavlović was a member of the General Secretariat of the delegation and Trumbić's secretary during the Conference. Diary of Stevan K Pavlović (in the Pavlović family possession), entry for 24 December 1918, hereafter Pavlović Diary.
5. 'Pashich, The Essence of Serbia' in Count Carlo Sforza, *Makers of Modern Europe: Portraits and Personal Impressions and Recollections* (Indianapolis: Bobbes-Merrill Co., 1930) pp 148–63.
6. Pavlowitch, *Serbia*, p 109.
7. Andrej Mitrović, *Jugoslavija na Konferenciji mira, 1919–1920* (Belgrade: Zavod z izdavanje adžbenika

Socijalističke Republike srbije, 1969) p 42, hereafter Mitrović, *Jugoslavija*.

8. Temperley, *History*, Vol 1, p 243–4.

9. Mitrović, *Jugoslavija*, p 6. A detailed breakdown of the delegation and an explanation of its structure and hierarchy is provided on pp 5–38.

10. See Temperley, *History*, Vol 1, pp 243–6.

11. Mitrović, *Jugoslavija*, p 14.

12. R G D Laffan, in Temperley, *History*, Vol 4, p 207.

13. Lederer, *Yugoslavia*, pp 93–4. For more on Cvijić's role see Mitrović, *Jugoslavija*, pp 84–90, and, more generally, on the role of Serbian intellectuals in the creation of Yugoslavia see Ljubinka Trgovčević, *Naučnici Srbije i stvaranje jugoslovenske države, 1914–1920* (Belgrade: SKZ, 1986) and 'South Slav Intellectuals and the Creation of Yugoslavia', in Dejan Djokić (ed), *Yugoslavism: Histories of a Failed Idea,1918–1992* (London: C Hurst, 2003) pp 222–37.

14. Lederer, *Yugoslavia*, p 84.

15. Lederer, *Yugoslavia*, p 91.

16. Count Carlo Sforza, *Fifty Years of War and Diplomacy in the Balkans: Pashich and the Union of the Yugoslavs* (New York: Columbia University Press, 1940) pp 146–7.

17. Smodlaka, *Zapisi*, p 115. Soon after the Yugoslav delegation started work, Pašić asked the government in Belgrade to send his son Radomir to help the work of the delegation and to backdate his payment to 9 January, 'as [with] all others'. Pavlović Diary, entry for 13 January 1919.

18. Harold Nicolson, *Peacemaking 1919* (London: Constable, 1933) p 253, hereafter Nicolson, *Peacemaking*.

19. Pavlović Diary, entries for 30 December 1918, 2 February 1919, and 13 January 1919.

20. 'Latin culture': Dragoljub Jovanović, *Ljudi, ljudi: Medaljoni 46 umrlih savremenika, sa fotografijama* (Belgrade: 1975), Vol 2, p 80, hereafter Jovanović, *Ljudi, ljudi*. 'Mingling': Smodlaka, *Zapisi*, pp 118–20.

21. Temperley, *History*, Vol 1, p 246.

22. *Zapisnici*, p 27 (translation by Lederer, *Yugoslavia*, p 123; I have used Lederer's translation of the minutes whenever it was available). For Smodlaka's relationship with Trumbić and Pašić see Smodlaka, *Zapisi*.

23. Margaret MacMillan, *Peacemakers: The Paris Peace Conference of 1919 and Its Attempt to End War* (London: John Murray, 2001) p 120, hereafter MacMillan, *Peacemakers*.

24. *Zapisnici*, p 27.

25. Lederer, *Yugoslavia*, p 125.

26. *Zapisnici*, p 28.

27. Lederer, *Yugoslavia*, p 126.

28. *Zapisnici*, pp 30–1.

29. Smodlaka, *Zapisi*, pp 120–1; 'Žolger's Secretariat': Mitrović, *Jugoslavija*, p 214; Uroš Lipušček, *Ave Wilson: ZDA in prekrajanje Slovenije v Versaillesu 1919–1920* (Ljubljana: Zal Sophia, 2003), deals in detail with the 'Slovene delegation' in Paris.

30. Paul Cambon, quoted in Sharp, *Versailles*, p 19.

6 Claims and Expectations

1. Smodlaka, *Jugoslav Territorial Claims*, p 10. See also *Memorandum presented to the Peace Conference, in Paris, concerning the Claims of the Kingdom of the*

Serbians, Croatians and Slovenes (Paris: 1919), and *The National Claims of the Serbians, Croatians and Slovenes* (Paris: 1919).

2. Lujo Vojnović [Count L. Voinovitch], *The Question of the Adriatic: Dalmatia* (Paris: 1919) and *The Question of the Adriatic: Fiume (Rieka)* (Paris: 1919).

3. Stephen Bonsal, *Suitors and Suppliants: The Little Nations at Versailles* (New York: Prentice Hall, 1946) p 247. Also cited in MacMillan, *Peacemakers*, p 120.

4. Cited in Lederer, *Yugoslavia*, p 10. For a recent analysis of the Italian national movement in the 19th century see Lucy Riall, *Risorgimento: The History of Italy from Napoleon to Nation State* (Basingstoke: Palgrave Macmillan, 2009).

5. Banac, *The National Question,* p 270.

6. Montenegrin support of the Corfu declaration: 'Deklaracija crnogorskog odbora za nar.[odno] ujedinjenje', Paris, 11 August (29 July O.S.), 1917, in Šišić, *Dokumenti*, p 100; 'Internal Serb affair': Banac, *The National Question*, pp 283–4.

7. See, for instance, Šerbo Rastoder, *Crna Gora u egzilu 1918–1925* (Podorica: 2004) 2 vols. King Nicholas died in exile in France in 1921. Plamenac eventually returned to Yugoslavia from exile and became a supporter of the regime. Hoover Institution Archives, Stanford University, Dragiša Cvetković Papers, Prince Paul folder, Plamenac to Prince Paul, Belgrade, 29 November 1938.
   8. *Zapisnici*, pp 21–2.

9. Lederer, *Yugoslavia*, pp 114–15.

10. *Zapisnici*, p 41.

11. Jovan Radonjić [Yovan Radonitch], *The Banat and the Serbo-Roumanian Frontier Problem* (Paris: 1919).

12. Brătianu's complaint: MacMillan, *Peacemakers*, p 140; British journalist: Henry Wickham Steed, *Through Thirty Years, 1892–1922: A Personal Narrative* 2 Vols (London: Heinemann, 1924) Vol 2, p 273.
13. Lederer, *Yugoslavia*, p 98.
14. *Zapisnici*, p 41.
15. Nicolson, *Peacemaking*, p 136.
16. *Zapisnici*, p 36.
17. All figures are round figures based on various, mostly Yugoslav documents that circulated at the Conference, helpfully summarised by Lederer, *Yugoslavia*, pp 100–1.
18. Bulgaria would temporarily regain Serbian Macedonia during the Second World War. In 1945 the region would once again return to Belgrade, but this time as a republic of socialist Yugoslavia. In 1992 Macedonia declared independence from Yugoslavia.
19. Slobodan Jovanović to Ivo Lederer, London, January-April 1955, Lederer, *Yugoslavia*, pp 91–2.
20. *Zapisnici*, pp 32–3.
21. *Zapisnici*, p 33.
22. *Zapisnici*, p 33.
23. Mitrović, *Jugoslavija*, pp 127–8, 169–76.
24. Lederer, *Yugoslavia*, p 102.
25. Even without taking into account a proposal for the establishment of a land corridor along the Austrian-Hungarian border that would link Czechoslovakia and Yugoslavia. This idea first emerged at the beginning of the First World War, among some Czech and Russian figures, and was discussed during the Paris Peace Conference, but was not in the end seriously considered.

7 War Crimes and War Guilt

1. Naoko Shimazu, *Japan, Race and Equality: The Racial Equality Proposal of 1919* (London: Routledge, 1998) pp 29–31. See also Mitrović, *Jugoslavija*, pp 64–70.

2. *Memorandum presented to the Peace Conference, in Paris, concerning the Claims of the Kingdom of the Serbians, Croatians and Slovenes* (Paris: 1919).

3. Milenko Vesnić, *O Društvu naroda* (Belgrade: Izdavačka Knjižarnica Gece Kona, 1920) pp 13–14, 17.

4. Sharp, *Versailles*, pp 133–6.

5. For different points of view, see Dwight E Lee (ed), *The Outbreak of the First World War: Who or What Was Responsible. Problems in European Civilization* (Lexington, MA: DC Heath, 1970). See also MacMillan, *Peacemakers*, pp 167–75; Sharp, *Versailles*, pp 90–1, 109–38; and Zara Steiner, *The Lights That Failed: European International History, 1919–1933* (Oxford: Oxford University Press, 2005) pp 59–67.

6. James F Willis, *Prologue to Nuremberg: The Politics and Diplomacy of Punishing War Criminals of the First World War* (Westport, CN: Greenwood, 1982) pp 148–50.

7. Figures for Serbia: Andrej Mitrović, *Srbija u Prvom svetskom ratu*, 2nd edn (Belgrade: Stubovi Kulture, 2004) p 509; for the Habsburg Yugoslavs: John R Lampe, *Yugoslavia as History: Twice There was a Country*, 2nd edn (Cambridge: Cambridge University Press, 2000) p 109. See Mitrović, *Great War*, esp. pp 221–32, for an account of oppression in occupied Serbia.

8. Mitrović, *Jugoslavija*, p 193.

9. Lampe, *Yugoslavia*, pp 108–9.

10. *Zapisnici*, p 48.

11. Sforza, *Makers of Modern Europe*, p 163.
12. R J Crampton, *The Makers of the Modern World: Aleksandŭr Stamboliĭski – Bulgaria* (London: Haus Publishing, 2009) p 77.
13. Mitrović, *Jugoslavija*, pp 194–5.
14. Mitrović, *Jugoslavija*, pp 195–9.
15. Willis, *Prologue*, p 153.

8 The Adriatic Question

1. Smodlaka, *Zapisi*, pp 113–14. The official minutes of the delegation do not include Pašić's monologues, but Smodlaka's account is plausible. Slobodan Jovanović wrote how Pašić would talk for hours and thus exhaust his political opponents into submission. Jovanović, 'Pašić', p 148.
2. *Zapisnici*, p 32.
3. *Zapisnici*, pp 38–9.
4. MacMillan, *Peacemakers*, p 120.
5. For a study of the Inquiry and for biographical information on the experts, see Lawrence E Gelfand, *The Inquiry: American Preparations for Peace, 1917–1919* (New Haven: Yale University Press, 1963), esp. chapters 2 and 7.
6. Lederer, *Yugoslavia*, pp 136–8, provides an excellent summary of the Inquiry and its influence on Wilson in respect of the Yugoslav question.
7. Lederer, *Yugoslavia*, p 142.
8. Cited in MacMillan, *Peacemakers*, p 298.
9. Lederer, *Yugoslavia*, pp 145–8.
10. *Zapisnici*, p 47n. Note that the Serbian delegates, as was the custom at the time, transliterated their surnames

from Cyrillic, rather than use the Serbo-Croat/Slovene Latin alphabet, as Trumbić and Žolger did.

11. Trumbić to the government, Paris, 13 February 1919, cited in Lederer, *Yugoslavia*, p 153.
12. *Zapisnici*, p 50.
13. *Zapisnici*, pp 51–4.
14. *Memorandum Presented to the Peace Conference, in Paris, Concerning the Claims of the Kingdom of the Serbians, Croatians and Slovenes* (Paris: 1919).
15. Lederer, *Yugoslavia*, p 158.
16. Cited in Lederer, *Yugoslavia*, p 159.
17. Lederer, *Yugoslavia*, pp 159–60.
18. Lederer, *Yugoslavia*, p 186.
19. *Zapisnici*, pp 91–2.
20. Cited in MacMillan, *Peacemakers*, p 120.
21. *Zapisnici*, p 108; Lederer, *Yugoslavia*, p 193.
22. *Zapisnici*, p 96; Lederer, *Yugoslavia*, pp 186–7.
23. *Zapisnici*, p 114; Lederer, *Yugoslavia*, p 194; Mitrović, *Jugoslavija*, p 120.
24. Lederer, *Yugoslavia*, p 202.
25. Mitrović, *Jugoslavija*, p 68.
26. 'Govor o rješenju Jadranskog pitanja u Općinskom kazalištu u Splitu, prosinca 1920. god', in Trumbić, *Izabrani politički spisi*, pp 180–91. For a neutral description of the Rapallo Conference and text of the Treaty, see Temperley, *History*, Vol 4, pp 327–37.

9 Settlements

1. Lederer, *Yugoslavia*, p 204.
2. For a brief but vivid description of the events preceding the signing of the Versailles Treaty and the ceremony itself see Temperley, *History*, Vol 2, pp 1–20.

3. Nicolson, *Peacemaking*, p 248.

4. Temperley, *History*, Vol 5, pp 147–8.

5. Texts of the Austrian treaty and the treaty on the protection of minorities between the Allied and Associated Powers and the Serb-Croat-Slovene state are reproduced in Temperley, *History*, Vol 5, pp 171–304 and 446–54, respectively. The Klagenfurt plebiscite figures: Temperley, *History*, Vol 4, p 379.

6. Temperley, *History*, Vol 5, pp 14, 374–5.

7. *Zapisnici*, p 126.

8. Lederer, *Yugoslavia*, p 256.

9. Temperley, *History*, Vol 4, p 212.

10. Lederer, *Yugoslavia*, pp 255–7; *Treaty of Peace between the Allied and Associated Powers and Bulgaria and Protocol, signed at Neuilly-sur-Seine, November 27, 1919* (London: 1920). Text of the Treaty is reproduced in Temperley, *History*, Vol 5, pp 305–65.

11. Mitrović, *Jugoslavija*, pp 179–80.

12. Lederer, *Yugoslavia*, pp 234–6; Mitrović, *Jugoslavija*, pp 138–40, 177–85.

13. *Zapisnici*, pp 288–9; Mitrović, *Jugoslavija*, pp 207–10.

14. *Zapisnici*, pp 301–2. Danilo Kalafatović, then a general, signed the Yugoslav Army's capitulation on 17 April 1941, at the end of Yugoslavia's short war against Nazi Germany, Fascist Italy and their allies. Thus, he participated in and witnessed both the birth and the death of the 'first' Yugoslavia.

10 Aftermath and Epilogue

1. During a conversation between Pašić, Trumbić, Clemenceau and Lloyd George in Paris on 20 January 1919. Smith Pavelić, *Trumbić*, pp 257–9.

2. All citations in this paragraph are from Ljubo Boban, 'Prilozi za političku biografiju Ante Trumbića u vrijeme šestojanuarskog režima (1929–35)', in Boban, *Kontroverze iz povijesti Jugoslavije*, 3 Vols (Zagreb: Školska Knjiga: Stvarnost, 1989) Vol 2, pp 15–87, p 28, hereafter Boban, *Kontroverze*.

3. Jovanović, 'Trumbić i Jugoslavija', in *Moji savremenici*, p 215.

4. Jovanović, 'Pašić' and 'Pašić i Jugoslavija', in *Moji savremenici*, pp 184 and 220, respectively.

5. Dragnich, *Serbia, Nikola Pašić and Yugoslavia*, p 163.

6. R W Seton-Watson, 'Jugoslav Obituary', *Slavonic Review*, Vol 19, No 53–54 (1939–40) pp 318–21, p 318.

7. Jovanović, *Ljudi, ljudi*, pp 79, 82.

8. 'Govor u Ustavotvornoj skupštini Kraljevine Srba, Hrvata i Slovenaca', 23 and 25 April 1921, in Trumbić, *Izabrani politički spisi*, p 195.

9. Ivo Petrinović, 'Politički život i nazori Ante Trumbića', in Trumbić, *Izabrani politički spisi*, pp 9–62, p 46.

10. Petrinović, 'Politički život i nazori Ante Trumbića', p 46.

11. Jovanović, *Ljudi, ljudi*, pp 80–1.

12. Boban, 'Prilozi za političku biografiju Ante Trumbića', pp 15–16. See also Ljubo Boban, 'Enes Milak i separatizam Ante Trumbića', in Boban, *Kontroverze*, Vol 1, pp 379–80.

13. For Trumbić's career during this period see Boban, 'Prilozi za političku biografiju Ante Trumbića'.

14. Prince Paul Papers, Bakhmeteff Archive, Columbia University, New York, box 11, Report on the reaction to the assassination [of King Alexander] in Croatia, unknown author, ca. late 1934.

15. Ivo J Lederer, 'Introduction', in Lederer (ed), *The Versailles Settlement: Was it Foredoomed to Failure? Problems in European Civilization* (Lexington, MA: Heath, 1960) pp vii–x, p vii, hereafter Lederer, 'Introduction'.

16. Bogoljub Kočović, *Žrtve Drugog svetskog rata u Jugoslaviji* (London: 1985), provides estimates of Yugoslav losses in the Second World War according to ethnicity.

17. Lederer, 'Introduction', pp vii-viii.

Chronology

YEAR	AGE (NP/AT)	THE LIFE AND THE LAND
1804		Karadjordje Petrović leads the first Serbian Uprising; Ottomans suppress the uprising in 1813.
1815		Miloš Obrenović leads the second Serbian Uprising. The previous year Vuk Karadžić publishes the first Serbian grammar in Vienna, followed by *Serbian Dictionary* (1818).
1830		Serbia achieves autonomy within the Ottoman Empire, under Miloš Obrenović as hereditary prince. Ljudevit Gaj, leader of the proto-Yugoslav Illyrian Movement, publishes *Short Basics of the Croatian-Slavonic Orthography* in Budapest.
1835		Serbia adopts first modern constitution. First theatre opens in Kragujevac, Serbia's capital. The Illyrians begin publishing their newspaper in Zagreb.
1841		The Illyrian Party and the pro-Hungarian Croatian-Hungarian Party founded in Croatia.
1842		'Defenders of the Constitution' in Serbia gain upper hand.

YEAR	HISTORY	CULTURE
1804	Napoleon Bonaparte becomes Emperor of France.	Beethoven, *Eroica* Symphony.
1815	The Hundred Days: Napoleon returns to France from exile in Elba, but is defeated at Waterloo and banished to St Helena. Otto von Bismarck born.	Sir Walter Scott, *Guy Mannering*. Canova, *The Three Graces*.
1830	Revolution in Paris: Louis-Philippe becomes King of France. Uprising in Warsaw against Russian rule. Franz Josef, future Austrian Emperor, born.	Delacroix, *Liberty Guiding the People*. Stendhal, *Le Rouge et le Noir*. William Cobbett, *Rural Rides*.
1835	Texas secedes from Mexico. First German railway line opens between Nuremberg and Furth.	William Wordsworth, *Poems*. Donizetti, *Lucia di Lammermoor*.
1841	British sovereignty declared over Hong Kong.	Charles Dickens, *The Old Curiosity Shop*. Saxophone invented.
1842	Webster-Ashburton Treaty between Great Britain and the USA defines Canadian frontier.	Edgar Allen Poe, *The Masque of the Red Death*. Wagner, *Rienzi*.

YEAR	AGE (NP/AT)	THE LIFE AND THE LAND
1844		Serbia's Interior Minister Ilija Garašanin writes *Načertanije* (Draft), on the country's national goals.
1845		December: Nikola Pašić born in Zaječar, eastern Serbia.
1848	3	Revolutions in Austria and throughout Europe; Croats and Serbs march on Budapest under the leadership of *ban* Josip Jelačić; 'Serb Vojvodina' temporarily established.
1850	5	The Vienna Literary Agreement lays the foundation of the Serbo-Croat language.
1861	16	Croatian Party of Rights formed.
1863	18	Belgrade National Theatre opens.
1864	19	17 May: Ante Trumbić born in Split, Dalmatia. Vuk Karadžić dies in Vienna.
1866	21/2	Pašić starts his degree at the Technical Faculty in Belgrade.

YEAR	HISTORY	CULTURE
1844	Treaty of Tangier ends French war in Morocco.	Alexandre Dumas père, *Le Comte de Monte Cristo*.
	China and US sign first treaty of peace, amity and commerce.	W M Thackeray, *Barry Lyndon*.
1845	First Maori War in New Zealand.	Edgar Allen Poe, *The Raven, and Other Poems*.
	First Sikh War begins.	
1848	France: revolt in Paris, Louis-Philippe abdicates, Louis Napoleon becomes President of French Republic.	Alexandre Dumas fils, *La Dame aux Camelias*.
		Karl Marx and Friedrich Engels issue *Communist Manifesto*.
	Vienna: uprising forces Metternich to resign.	John Everett Millais, *Ophelia*.
1850	Peace of Berlin between Prussia and Denmark over Schleswig-Holstein.	Ivan Turgenev, *A Month in the Country*.
		Public Libraries Act in Britain.
1861	Confederate States of America formed: US Civil War begins.	Charles Dickens, *Great Expectations*.
1863	US Civil War: Confederate defeats at Gettysburg and Vicksburg, Lincoln's 'Gettysburg Address'.	Charles Kingsley, *The Water Babies*.
		Football Association founded, London.
1864	Schleswig War: Austrian and Prussian troops defeat Danes.	Leo Tolstoy, *War and Peace* (– 1869).
1866	Austro-Prussian War: Prussian victory at Sadowa, end of German Confederation.	Fyodor Dostoevsky, *Crime and Punishment*.
	Revolts in Crete against Turkish rule.	

YEAR	AGE (NP/AT)	THE LIFE AND THE LAND
1867	22/3	Last Ottoman soldiers leave Serbia.
		Austro-Hungarian Compromise.
		The Yugoslav Academy of Sciences and Arts founded in Zagreb.
1868	23/4	Assassination of Prince Michael of Serbia.
		Hungarian-Croatian Compromise.
		Pašić continues his studies at the Federal Polytechnic Institute, Zurich.
1875	30/11	Uprising of Herzegovinian and Bosnian peasants. Serbia and Montenegro declare war on the Ottoman Empire.
1876–7	31–32/ 12–13	Serbia defeated. Russia declares war on the Ottoman Empire, Serbia and Montenegro join Russia.
1878	33/14	Ottomans defeated.
		March: San Stefano Treaty establishes a Greater Bulgaria.
		Jun–Jul: Congress of Berlin: Serbia and Montenegro independent. Austria-Hungary occupies Bosnia-Herzegovina; San Stefano Treaty annulled.
1881	36/17	Pašić elected leader of the newly founded People's Radical Party, the first modern party in Serbia. Treaty between Austria-Hungary and Serbia.

YEAR	HISTORY	CULTURE
1867	French abandon Maximilian in Mexico: executed soon after. Dominion of Canada established. North German Confederation founded.	Anthony Trollope, *The Last Chronicle of Barset*. Émile Zola, *Thérèse Raquin*. Karl Marx, *Das Kapital* Vol I.
1868	British Abyssinian expedition. Meiji Restoration in Japan. Ulysses S Grant elected US President.	Louisa May Alcott, *Little Women*. Wilkie Collins, *The Moonstone*. Richard Wagner, *Die Meistersänger von Nürnberg*.
1875	Prince of Wales visits India. Britain buys Suez Canal shares from Khedive of Egypt.	Mark Twain, *The Adventures of Tom Sawyer*. Gilbert and Sullivan, *Trial by Jury*.
1876–7	Ottoman sultan deposed. New Ottoman constitution proclaimed. Queen Victoria proclaimed Empress of India.	First complete performance of Wagner's 'Ring Cycle' at Bayreuth. Henry James, *The American*.
1878	Electric street lighting introduced in London.	Thomas Hardy, *The Return of the Native*. Ruskin-Whistler libel case.
1881	First Boer War. US President Garfield assassinated. Pogroms against the Jews in Russia.	Henry James, *Portrait of a Lady*. Offenbach, *Les Contes d'Hoffmann*.

YEAR	AGE (NP/AT)	THE LIFE AND THE LAND
1882	37/18	Serbia becomes a kingdom, under Milan Obrenović. Trumbić starts Law degree at the University of Zagreb, and two years later continues his studies in Vienna and Graz.
1883	38/19	Peasant uprising in eastern Serbia. Pašić flees to Bulgaria, sentenced to death *in absentia*. Budapest appoints Károly Khuen-Héderváry as *ban* (governor) of Croatia.
1885	40/21	Serbo-Bulgarian war. Serbia defeated, but saved from the Bulgarian invasion by Austria-Hungary.
1889	44/25	King Milan abdicates; Pašić returns from exile and is elected president of the Serbian parliament the same year. The 500th anniversary of the Battle of Kosovo commemorated in Belgrade and Zagreb.
1890	45/26	Pašić elected mayor of Belgrade; marries Djurdjina Duković in Florence. Trumbić graduates; awarded a doctorate.
1891	46/27	Pašić appointed Prime Minister for the first time; resigns the following year.

YEAR	HISTORY	CULTURE
1882	Triple Alliance between Italy, Germany and Austria-Hungary. British occupy Cairo. Hiram Maxim patents his machine gun.	R L Stevenson, *Treasure Island*. Leslie Stephen, *Science of Ethics*. Wagner, *Parsifal*. Tchaikovsky, *1812 Overture*.
1883	The French gain control of Tunis. British decide to evacuate the Sudan. The Orient Express (Paris-Constantinople) makes its first run.	Nietzsche, *Thus Spake Zarathustra*.
1885	The Congo becomes the personal possession of King Léopold II of Belgium. Germany annexes Tanganyika and Zanzibar.	Maupassant, *Bel Ami*. H Rider Haggard, *King Solomon's Mines*.
1889	Austro-Hungarian Crown Prince Rudolf commits suicide at Mayerling.	Jerome K Jerome, *Three Men in a Boat*. Richard Strauss, *Don Juan*.
1890	Bismarck dismissed by Wilhelm II. German Social Democrats adopt Marxist Erfurt Programme.	Oscar Wilde, *The Picture of Dorian Gray*. Mascagni, *Cavelleria Rusticana*. First moving picture shows in New York.
1891	Triple Alliance (Austria-Hungary, Germany, Italy) renewed for 12 years. Franco-Russian entente.	Thomas Hardy, *Tess of the D'Urbervilles*. Mahler, *Symphony No 1*.

YEAR	AGE (NP/AT)	THE LIFE AND THE LAND
1892	47/28	Josip Broz Tito, leader of the communist Yugoslavia, born in Kumrovec, Croatia. Ivo Andrić, the only Yugoslav Nobel Prize laureate, born in Travnik, Bosnia.
1893	48/29	King Alexander Obrenović carries out a *coup d'état*. First tram line opens in Belgrade; the following year the city authorities install electric street lamps: in Jun 1896 the first cinema opens in Belgrade.
1897	52/33	Trumbić elected deputy in the Austrian parliament.
1898	53/34	Pašić arrested for his criticism of the Obrenović dynasty.
1899	54/35	Pašić accused of plotting against the life of King Milan; saved from execution by Russia and Austria-Hungary.
1903	58/39	Assassination of King Alexander and Queen Draga of Serbia. Peter Karadjordjević assumes throne. Croatian *ban* Khuen-Héderváry leaves office.

YEAR	HISTORY	CULTURE
1915	First World War: Battles of Neuve Chappelle and Loos. The 'Shells Scandal'. Germans sink the British liner *Lusitania,* killing 1,198. Armenian deportations begin as Russian army advances into eastern Turkey.	Nobel Prize in Literature: Romain Rolland (France). Joseph Conrad, *Victory.* John Buchan, *The Thirty-Nine Steps.* Ezra Pound, *Cathay.* Film: *The Birth of a Nation.*
1916	First World War. Western Front: Battle of Verdun, France. The Battle of the Somme. The Battle of Jutland. US President Woodrow Wilson is re-elected. Wilson issues Peace Note to belligerents in European war. Lloyd George becomes Prime Minister.	Nobel Prize in Literature: V von Heidenstam (Sweden). James Joyce, *Portrait of an Artist as a Young Man.* Film: *Intolerance.*
1917	First World War. February Revolution in Russia. USA declares war on Germany.	Nobel Prize in Literature: Karl Gjellerup & H Pontoppidan (Denmark). T S Eliot, *Prufrock and Other Observations.*

YEAR	AGE (NP/AT)	THE LIFE AND THE LAND
1918	73/54	29 Oct: Zagreb: State of Slovenes, Croats and Serbs proclaimed.
		26 Nov: Podgorica: unification of Montenegro and Serbia proclaimed in parliament.
		Dec: Belgrade: Prince Regent Alexander of Serbia proclaims the Kingdom of Serbs, Croats, and Slovenes, but blocks Pašić's choice as prime minister; Trumbić appointed foreign minister.
1919	74/55	Jan: Pašić heads the delegation of the Kingdom of Serbs, Croats and Slovenes at the Peace Conference in Paris, with Trumbić as his deputy; the Conference refuses to recognise the delegation under its full name, referring to the new country as 'Serbia'.
		7 Feb: US recognises the Kingdom of Serbs, Croats, and Slovenes, but not its peace delegation.
		7 May: draft German Treaty refers to 'Serbia-Croatia-Slavonia' [sic]; 2 and 6 Jun: Britain and France recognise the new kingdom, respectively.
		28 Jun: Pašić, Trumbić and Vesnić sign the Treaty of Versailles as plenipotentiaries of the Serb-Croat-Slovene Kingdom.
		27 Nov: Treaty of Neuilly with Bulgaria signed.
		5 Dec: Pašić, Trumbić and Žolger sign the Treaty of St Germain.

YEAR	HISTORY	CULTURE
1918	First World War.	Alexander Blok, *The Twelve.*
	Peace Treaty of Brest-Litovsk between Russia and the Central Powers.	Gerald Manley Hopkins, *Poems.*
		Luigi Pirandello, *Six Characters in Search of an Author.*
	Romania signs Peace of Bucharest with Germany and Austria-Hungary.	Bela Bartok, *Bluebeard's Castle.*
		Puccini, *Il Trittico.*
	Ex-Tsar Nicholas II and family executed.	Gustav Cassel, *Theory of Social Economy.*
	Armistice signed between Allies and Germany; German Fleet surrenders.	Kokoshka, *Friends* and *Saxonian Landscape.*
		Edvard Munch, *Bathing Man.*
	Kaiser Wilhelm II of Germany abdicates.	
1919	Communist Revolt in Berlin.	Nobel Prize in Literature: Carl Spitteler (Switzerland).
	Paris Peace Conference adopts principle of founding League of Nations.	Bauhaus movement founded by Walter Gropius.
	Benito Mussolini founds Fascist movement in Italy.	Thomas Hardy, *Collected Poems.*
	Irish War of Independence begins.	George Bernard Shaw, *Heartbreak House.*
	US Senate votes against ratification of Versailles Treaty, leaving the USA outside the League of Nations.	Film: *The Cabinet of Dr Caligari.*

YEAR	AGE (NP/AT)	THE LIFE AND THE LAND
1920	75/56	Jun: Pašić resigns as head of the peace delegation; the government discharges the delegation in July.
		4 Jun: Treaty of Trianon with Hungary signed. 10 Aug: Treaty of Sèvres with the Ottoman Empire signed.
		Nov: Rapallo Treaty settles the dispute between Italy and Yugoslavia. Trumbić resigns as foreign minister; first general elections in Yugoslavia: Radicals come second behind the Democrats; Trumbić elected to parliament as an independent candidate.
1921	76/57	Pašić elected prime minister, remains in office for most of the following five years (1921–4, 1924–6).
		28 Jun: First Constitution of the Kingdom of Serbs, Croats and Slovenes adopted; the centralist Constitution is supported by Pašić, but opposed by Trumbić.
1923		Mar: the Radicals win the general elections comfortably; the Croatian Peasant Party comes second.

YEAR	HISTORY	CULTURE
1920	League of Nations comes into existence.	Nobel Prize in Literature: Knut Hamsun (Norway).
	The Hague is selected as seat of International Court of Justice.	F Scott Fitzgerald, *This Side of Paradise*.
	League of Nations headquarters moved to Geneva.	Franz Kafka, *The Country Doctor*.
	Warren G Harding wins US Presidential election.	Katherine Mansfield, *Bliss*.
	Bolsheviks win Russian Civil War.	Rambert School of Ballet formed.
	Government of Ireland Act passed.	Vincent D'Indy, *The Legend Of St Christopher*.
	Adolf Hitler announces his 25-point programme in Munich.	Maurice Ravel, *La Valse*.
1921	Irish Free State established.	Nobel Prize in Literature: Anatole France (France).
	Peace treaty signed between Russia and Germany.	Aldous Huxley, *Chrome Yellow*.
	State of Emergency proclaimed in Germany in the face of economic crisis.	D H Lawrence, *Women in Love*.
		Prokofiev, *The Love for Three Oranges*.
	Washington Naval Treaty signed.	
1923	French and Belgian troops occupy the Ruhr when Germany fails to make reparation payments.	Nobel Prize in Literature: W B Yeats (Ireland).
		George Gershwin, *Rhapsody in Blue*.
	The USSR formally comes into existence.	Max Beckmann, *The Trapeze*.
	23 Jul: Peace is signed at Lausanne.	Bela Bartok, *Dance Suite*.

YEAR	AGE (NP/AT)	THE LIFE AND THE LAND
1924	79/60	Trumbić joins the Croatian Bloc. Pašić briefly out of office.
1925	80/61	Feb: the Radicals gain further seats in the general elections, the Croatian Peasants come second again. July: the Pašić–Radić agreement. Croatian Peasant Party enters government.
1926	81/62	Jan: Trumbić forms the Croatian Federalist Peasant Party. 10 Dec: Pašić dies in Belgrade.
1927		Sep: the last democratic elections in inter-war Yugoslavia; the Radicals and the Croatian Peasants remain the two strongest parties, respectively. Trumbić reelected to parliament.
1928	64	20 Jun: Assassination of Croat deputies in the Belgrade parliament by a Radical deputy, 2 killed and 3 wounded, including Stjepan Radić; Radić dies on 8 Aug. Trumbić joins the Croatian Peasant Party.

YEAR	HISTORY	CULTURE
1924	Death of Lenin. Dawes Plan published. Greece is proclaimed a republic.	Nobel Prize in Literature: Wladyslaw S Reymot (Poland). E M Forster, *A Passage to India*.
1925	Pound Sterling returns to the Gold Standard. In Italy, Mussolini announces that he will take dictatorial powers. Locarno Treaty signed in London.	Nobel Prize in Literature: George Bernard Shaw (Ireland). Virginia Woolf, *Mrs Dalloway*. Film: *Battleship Potemkin*.
1926	General Strike in Great Britain. Germany is admitted into the League of Nations.	Nobel Prize in Literature: Grazia Deledda (Italy). Ernest Hemingway, *The Sun Also Rises*. Film: *The General*.
1927	Inter-Allied military control of Germany ends. Britain recognises rule of Ibn Saud in the Hejaz.	Nobel Prize in Literature: Henri Bergson (France). Marcel Proust, *Le Temps retrouve*. Film: *The Jazz Singer*.
1928	Italian electorate is reduced from ten million to three million. Kellogg-Briand Pact outlawing war and providing for peaceful settlement of disputes, is signed. Albania is proclaimed a Kingdom.	Nobel Prize in Literature: Sigrid Undset (Norway). D H Lawrence, *Lady Chatterley's Lover*. Henri Matisse, *Seated Odalisque*. George Gershwin, *An American in Paris*.

YEAR	AGE (NP/AT)	THE LIFE AND THE LAND
1929	65	6 Jan: King Alexander introduces a dictatorship. 3 Oct: Country renamed Yugoslavia, new administrative provinces (*banovinas*) introduced. Ante Pavelić forms the *Ustaša* organisation in Italy.
1931	67	King Alexander grants new constitution, but Yugoslavia remains a dictatorship.
1932	68	Nov: The 'Zagreb Points'; Trumbić one of the authors of the manifesto.
1934	70	9 Oct: King Alexander assassinated in Marseilles by a Macedonian revolutionary working for the *Ustašas*; Alexander's first cousin, Prince Paul rules in the name of minor King Peter II.

YEAR	HISTORY	CULTURE
1929	Fascists win single-party elections in Italy. Germany accepts Young Plan at Reparations Conference in the Hague – Allies agree to evacuate the Rhineland. Wall Street Crash.	Nobel Prize in Literature: Thomas Mann (Germany). Erich Remarque, *All Quiet on the Western Front.* Piet Mondrian, *Composition with Yellow and Blue.*
1931	Bankruptcy of Credit-Anstalt in Austria begins financial collapse of Central Europe.	Nobel Prize in Literature: Erik Axel Karlfeldt (Sweden). Robert Frost, *Collected Poems.*
1932	Germany withdraws temporarily from the Geneva Disarmament Conference. F D Roosevelt wins US Presidential election.	Nobel Prize in Literature: John Galsworthy (Great Britain). Pablo Picasso, *Head of a Woman.*
1934	Germany, 'Night of the Long Knives'. Hitler becomes *Führer.* USSR admitted to League of Nations. Japan repudiates Washington treaties of 1922 and 1930.	Nobel Prize in Literature: John Galsworthy (Great Britain). Jean Cocteau, *La Machine Infernale* Film: *David Copperfield.*

YEAR	AGE (NP/AT)	THE LIFE AND THE LAND
1935	71	May: Quasi-democratic general elections. Croatian Peasant Party participates jointly with the Serbian opposition parties, but the Serb-Croat coalition fails to oust the Serb-dominated government. Trumbić opposes the cooperation between the Croatian Peasants and the Serb parties.
1937	73	Oct: Bloc of the National Agreement of Croat and Serb opposition parties.
1938	74	18 Nov: Trumbić dies in Split.
1939		Aug: Croatia granted autonomy by Belgrade; Maček appointed Deputy Prime Minister of Yugoslavia.

YEAR	HISTORY	CULTURE
1935	Prime Ministers of Italy, France and Britain issue protest at German rearmament and agree to act together against Germany. Hoare-Laval Pact. Hitler announces anti-Jewish 'Nuremberg Laws'. League of Nations imposes sanctions against Italy following its invasion of Abyssinia.	George Gershwin, *Porgy and Bess.* Richard Strauss, *Die Schweigsame Frau.* T S Eliot, *Murder in the Cathedral.* Emlyn Williams, *Night Must Fall.* Ivy Compton-Burnett, *A House and its Head.* Film: *The 39 Steps.*
1937	UK royal commission on Palestine recommends partition into British and Arab areas and Jewish state. Italy joins German-Japanese Anti-Comintern Pact.	Nobel Prize in Literature: Roger Martin du Gard (France). Jean-Paul Sartre, *Nausea.* John Steinbeck, *Of Mice and Men.* Film: *A Star is Born.*
1938	German troops enter Austria, which is declared part of the German Reich.	Nobel Prize in Literature: Pearl Buck (USA). Film: *Alexander Nevsky.*
1939	Italy invades Albania. Pact of Steel signed by Hitler and Mussolini. German invasion of Poland: Britain and France declare war. Soviets invade Finland.	Nobel Prize in Literature: Frans Eemil Sillanpää (Finland). Bela Bartok, *String Quartet No. 6.* Film: *Gone with the Wind.*

YEAR	AGE (NP/AT)	THE LIFE AND THE LAND
1941		25 Mar: Yugoslavia joins the Tripartite Pact; popular protests against the Pact.
		27 Mar: Military coup in Belgrade; Prince Paul and his government deposed; Peter II proclaimed of age.
		6 Apr: Nazi Germany and Fascist Italy lead an attack on Yugoslavia. Belgrade heavily bombed.
		10 Apr: Independent State of Croatia proclaimed in Zagreb, under the *Ustaša* puppet regime; the king and the government flee the country before, on 17 Apr, General Kalafatović (a member of the Serb-Croat-Slovene delegation in Paris), signs capitulation; the end of the 'first' Yugoslavia.

John R Lampe, *Yugoslavia as History: Twice there was a Country* (Cambridge: Cambridge University Press, revised and expanded edn 2000). Stevan K Pavlowitch's *Yugoslavia* (London: Benn, 1971) and *Improbable Survivor: Yugoslavia and Its Problems, 1918–1988* (London: Hurst, 1989) are both excellent and still invaluable, as is his somewhat underrated *A History of the Balkans, 1804–1945* (London: Longman, 1999). Charles and Barbara Jelavich, *The Establishment of the Balkan National States, 1804–1920* (Seattle: University of Washington Press, 1977) remains useful. Finally, Dejan Djokić and James Ker-Lindsay (eds), *New Perspectives on Yugoslavia: Key Issues and Controversies* (London: Routledge, 2010) hopefully complements these general works.

Picture Sources

The author and publishers wish to express their thanks to the following sources of illustrative material and/or permission to reproduce it. They will make proper acknowledgements in future editions in the event that any omissions have occurred.

Illustrations courtesy of Topham Picturepoint.

Endpapers
The Signing of Peace in the Hall of Mirrors, Versailles, 28th June 1919 by Sir William Orpen (Imperial War Museum: Bridgeman Art Library)
Front row: Dr Johannes Bell (Germany) signing with Herr Hermann Müller leaning over him
Middle row (seated, left to right): General Tasker H Bliss, Col E M House, Mr Henry White, Mr Robert Lansing, President Woodrow Wilson (United States); M Georges Clemenceau (France); Mr David Lloyd George, Mr Andrew Bonar Law, Mr Arthur J Balfour, Viscount Milner, Mr G N Barnes (Great Britain); Prince Saionji (Japan)
Back row (left to right): M Eleftherios Venizelos (Greece);

Dr Afonso Costa (Portugal); Lord Riddell (British Press);
Sir George E Foster (Canada); M Nikola Pašić (Serbia);
M Stephen Pichon (France); Col Sir Maurice Hankey,
Mr Edwin S Montagu (Great Britain); the Maharajah of
Bikaner (India); Signor Vittorio Emanuele Orlando (Italy);
M Paul Hymans (Belgium); General Louis Botha (South
Africa); Mr W M Hughes (Australia)

Jacket images

(Front): Imperial War Museum: akg Images.
(Back): *Peace Conference at the Quai d'Orsay* by Sir William
Orpen (Imperial War Museum: akg Images).
Left to right (seated): Signor Orlando (Italy); Mr Robert
Lansing, President Woodrow Wilson (United States); M
Georges Clemenceau (France); Mr David Lloyd George, Mr
Andrew Bonar Law, Mr Arthur J Balfour (Great Britain);
Left to right (standing): M Paul Hymans (Belgium); Mr
Eleftherios Venizelos (Greece); The Emir Feisal (The
Hashemite Kingdom); Mr W F Massey (New Zealand);
General Jan Smuts (South Africa); Col E M House (United
States); General Louis Botha (South Africa); Prince Saionji
(Japan); Mr W M Hughes (Australia); Sir Robert Borden
(Canada); Mr G N Barnes (Great Britain); M Ignacy
Paderewski (Poland)

Index